THE
WATERMELON
KING

BY

DANIEL ROYSE

a
STATE39
publication

ISBN: 0692491724
ISBN-13: 9780692491720

For Ken and Kay Royse.

ACKNOWLEDGMENTS

I'd like to thank the following people for their help in
making this book a reality.

Ken Royse
Kay Royse
Suzy Royse
James Royse
Shannon Ito

TABLE OF CONTENTS

PREFACE

The Watermelon King is as much about backpacking across Africa as it is about rural North Dakota in the late 20th century. The story draws parallels between the experiences of different generations and shows how the actions of one person can affect the actions of another.

Though most of the story takes place in isolated corners of East Africa, *The Watermelon King* highlights a forgotten period of rural American life and shows how it can still be pertinent today.

I use the term "inspired by true events" because this story is based on a solo-backpacking trip that I did in 2009. However for the purpose of the story I needed to pick and choose actual events that occurred over a larger time frame and greater geographical area, and use them strategically throughout the storyline. The short stories written by my father are true and accurate accounts to the best of our knowledge. Those short stories have not been changed in any significant way aside from the names of the people involved.

It is important to note that even though some family members are written about in great detail while others have been left out completely, this was not meant to imply any greater significance to their achievements over others. In the end it came down to what information was available and the need to create a concise storyline by limiting the scope of the book.

Also, I must note that if my depiction of Africa,

Ethiopia or Kenya is in anyway perceived as derogatory it is not because I dislike or look down upon those countries or cultures. It is merely my attempt at an authentic representation of my feelings and emotions during my travels through the region.

CHAPTER 1
ROOM FOR RENT

Friday the 13th, February 2009. It started like any day before it. Even at 28 years old I had a pretty predicable routine in place. It was comfortable, normal, and with time, became easy. Twice a day, like a zombie in headphones, I would ride the N train between my apartment on Haight Street and downtown San Francisco. I would stand in the corner with my back against the door facing the flow of passengers and do my best to avoid any unnecessary conversation. This was how I started and ended each day. My daily commute was my little corner of the world and it was rare to stray outside that three-mile stretch of metro line.

I wasn't alone though, not really. Each day I would see the same people on the train. Every one of them with the same tired, bored look. Each one knowing that they just needed to get though another week until that glorious weekend arrived where they could sleep in, get wasted or just sit on the couch and stare at the television. We rode together every day and never said a word to each other. It was our chance to wake up, unwind, to think, to un-think…just a few glorious moments where nothing needed to be done.

But this Friday was different. It was the middle of the afternoon and I was on the train three hours ahead of every body else. The workday was still in full swing and I had the train nearly all to myself. There were a few stragglers, however. A Mexican woman with a push-cart of groceries, some high school kids ditching class, a young guy in a full suit who was probably on his way to a job interview, and a homeless man who was attempting to fix what I could only assume was the world's last remaining "Walkman".

In the corner seat along the wall I sat staring at my reflection in the glass on the opposite side of the train. I was dressed in full business attire and feeling out of place as I left the financial district on that infamously unlucky Friday afternoon. Holding a cardboard box filled with a notebook, a coffee mug and a small Aloe Vera plant peeking out from the top, my situation would have been obvious at first glance. Like so many others at that time, I had lost my job in the economic collapse that started a year before.

Yesterday, I was a consultant at one of the world's largest professional services firms. Yesterday, I woke up early and exhausted. I put on a suit and slacks and drank my daily coffee. Yesterday, I spent the day in meeting rooms, sending emails and eating lunch at my desk. Yesterday was the same as every day before it. But today, tomorrow, these days were uncertain.

My first instinct was to do the practical thing. I thought that I would take a week off, relax a bit and start applying for new and better jobs; try to make the best of a bad situation. There was of course, no way I could afford to live in San Francisco very long without working. But still, I couldn't shake the relentless sound of my younger sister's voice in the back of my head, urging me to take the road less practical.

"When will you get another chance like this? You have your whole life to sit at a desk," I could hear her say.

She was always the person to challenge me when I started to think too much like an "adult", in the end saving me from making those small sacrifices for the sake of security that inevitably end up leading us into a life of premature normalcy. Sometimes a dose of youthful optimism can be helpful when we become too afraid of losing what we have.

Maybe it helped that unlike most people, I didn't really mind getting laid off. Perhaps I even welcomed it a bit. I didn't have a mortgage to pay off. I didn't have a wife or kids to support. I didn't even have a loan on my car. I was a free man, and an excuse was all I needed to do something, anything different. I had lived abroad in the past and it was starting to feel like it was time to get back out into the world again.

As usual, I took the train to my stop at Dubose Park and continued to walk the remaining few blocks to my apartment. It was a cold day in San Francisco, but then again everyday was cold in San Francisco. On top of the normal bone chilling wind and fog, that day had the added annoyance of a light rain that came in from the side and made my shabby, little umbrella utterly useless. Luckily, my apartment was only three blocks from where the train dropped me off and the tall Victorian houses made a good shelter from the side-ways rain as I made my way home.

My apartment sat above an Iraqi restaurant called "Baghdad Nights" on Haight Street. It was just a few blocks from where the hippie movement of the 1960's began and it still maintained a lot of that bohemian character. Both my apartment and the restaurant below were owned and operated by a cheerful Iraqi guy who had made his home in San Francisco after being captured by the US military during the war in Iraq. He loved the United States and especially San Francisco, but I could always tell that a part of him missed his homeland and the culture he grew up with.

In typical San Francisco fashion, our apartment was long, narrow and built in the standard Victorian style architecture. The entrance to the apartment was at street level and was guarded with a steel gate to keep out the general riffraff that liked to call Haight Street home. A staircase leading up to the top floor turned into a hallway with rooms attached on one side and continued to stretch all the way to the back living room at the far end of the apartment.

Over the years we had managed to fill the place with all sorts of odd-looking décor: high ceilings plastered with strange art, an antique dinner table, a tree, beanbag chairs and sofas, a beer brewing station and even a hot tub. This was actually a very natural process for us as it's typical in San Francisco for people to leave unwanted furniture on street corners where it inevitably gets picked up by the next person who doesn't want to go through the hassle of renting a car and driving out to Ikea for a new coffee table. When you're ready to upgrade, you simply "give it back to the street" and the cycle continues. On Haight Street in particular, items wouldn't usually last more than 30 minutes before they were claimed.

Another typical feature of San Francisco living is the need to have multiple people sharing a single apartment. We had a total of six in ours, each person with their own room. An immediate indication of this would have been the number of bicycles hanging from the walls as you walked in. Although, for some reason we had eight of them.

The roommates in the house were a mix of people from all walks of life, but there were similarities among all of us. We were all young, transient and recently new to the city. Most of the roommates would stay an average of about a year; at which time the remaining roommates would post an ad to fill the newly vacant space. Competition for housing in San Francisco was fierce and our apartment was no exception. For each ad we posted online we would receive about 120 responses, each of them desperately trying to sell themselves to gain a spot in our centrally located San Francisco apartment, for which I was the lease holder.

As I made my way into our living room, I placed my

cardboard box on the kitchen table. The apartment was quiet as everyone was still at work and the only sound to be heard was the relentless wind shaking the old Victorian windows. It was in that moment that it occurred to me that the next ad posted for a roommate would be my replacement.

CHAPTER 2
BOLLOCKS

"Hey man."

"Yeah?"

"What's with all the guns…in the street…in the middle of the day?" Ethan said nervously.

"Not sure, might be a demonstration or something."

From inside the taxi we could see the street in front of us begin to fill with people. Slowly, this mob began to move west across the road, swelling in size at the intersection and blocking any movement forward. As more people filled the intersection, it became impossible for our car to pull ahead as we became engulfed by the sudden influx of bodies. The mob mostly consisted of young men, many of them waving AK47's or flags and cheering in a language we couldn't understand. Whatever they were chanting, there was passion in their voices and my only concern was whether this was a celebration or a protest. As an outsider, it wasn't so easy to tell.

"Okay, but why are they swarming around our taxi?"

"Relax, they're swarming around all the cars…not just ours."

I could tell Ethan was starting to get nervous, and understandably so. It was, after all, his first day in Africa and he had only been outside the airport now for a total of 20 minutes. He had flown into Bole International Airport, which was located on the south side of town. Our hotel was on the north side and getting there was the first item on our agenda.

Seconds after I responded to his question in my best calm-and-confident tone of voice, one of the men outside carrying an AK47 noticed us sitting in the back of the taxi. Amongst the yelling and the waving of guns, he immediately stopped his involvement and turned to point his gun in our direction from outside the taxi window. He raised his eyebrows and his eyes locked with mine.

Ethan turned even whiter than usual as the blood rushed from his face and silence fell over the car. This was a poor introduction to a great country, but sometimes these things are hard to avoid. Bad luck, really.

From inside the taxi, I was able to look directly at the man who had the Kalashnikov pointed between my eyes. He wore a red t-shirt with the slogan "Just Do It" plastered across his chest. His tore up blue jeans hung loosely over his black plastic sandals, but the real standout item was the semi-automatic weapon in this hands. After a moment had passed and with a burst of optimism, I simply smiled and waved at him. Within an instant he smiled back, yelled something toward the passing crowd and returned his attention to the chaos unfolding outside. As it turned out, this was not a violent protest. Despite the unnerving amount of weaponry in the crowd, this was a celebration of sorts.

Once our driver was able to crawl in and out of the intersection and away from the madness of the crowd, we were able to travel with relative ease the rest of the way to our hotel. Normally a demonstration like this would have prompted me to stop and take a few photos, but we wanted to get settled into our hotel before starting our exploration of the city.

It was nice to finally have some company out here in Africa, and this was the first time my brother and I had traveled together. We had a lot of time in front of us, but our journey started here in Addis Ababa, Ethiopia's ancient capital city; otherwise known simply as "Addis".

As we sped down Bole Road, one of the cities' main arteries, I could see Ethan's amazement as he watched the scenery fly by. Over the cracked asphalt streets, we passed by small pockets of people in markets doing their daily shopping, street vendors selling food and the crumbling cement storefronts of tire shops, cell phone dealers and tiny convenience stores that seemed to dot the city landscape. Every so often we'd pass by a pack of stray dogs searching for food or a group of kids in the distance playing with a variety of makeshift toys. Sprinkled in a seemingly random fashion along our path were a number of upscale coffee shops, bars, clubs and outdoor cafes. Brand new buildings were being put up right next to others that were falling apart…an indicator of an emerging middle class in the capital city, or a lack of city planning.

The city itself was perpetually loud as the sounds of honking, yelling and engines revving filled the air. On the road itself, it was a messy combination of cars, vans, buses, rickshaws and motorbikes all desperately fighting with one another to reach their respective destinations. The energy made the city feel wild like an urban jungle unlike anything in the States. Above it all drifted a perpetual cloud of exhaust fumes that blanketed the city each day, which by now I hardly noticed.

A few days before Ethan's arrival, I checked into a small hotel off of De Gaulle Square where I had stayed a few weeks prior. It was a basic place with a few rooms and a restaurant that served good Ethiopian food and strong coffee. The hotel staff didn't speak much English, but they were friendly and almost always lounging around within shooting distance of the front desk. Overall there was really nothing special about the place aside from the fact that I knew it existed. Our room consisted of two small twin beds, a window and a single nightstand between us. On the wall hung a dilapidated poster of a girl in a bikini holding a bottle of Bud Light. Our bathroom was down the hall and was a situation where flip-flops would be required at all times.

The downside of many budget hotels in Addis, this one included, is that they tended to be rent-by-the-hour establishments, otherwise known as brothels. Yes, it's a little grimy but when you're backpacking you do whatever you can to save a buck. Besides, I didn't think Ethan would mind; in fact, I figured it was unlikely that he would even notice.

Our taxi driver dropped us off and we paid him our pre-negotiated fare plus a small tip. Ethan got out and looked dizzily around as he tried to orientate himself with the new surroundings. The sights and smells were only slightly less chaotic than the ride over. We made our way up a small set of wooden stairs and across a patio, at the end of which was a pair of two large doors that led into the hotel lobby. As we stood at the front desk of the hotel, I began to explain to the receptionist that there would now be two of us staying in the room. This of course, resulted in a small additional fee. Ethan, as expected, said nothing about the dingy accommodation as he was entirely focused on the two girls staring at us from the lobby sofa. They were dressed in brightly colored mini skirts and appeared to be just as interested in him.

"Hey, let's go!" I said, as I pushed him in the direction of our room.

"Ah okay," he said, as if being awoken from a trance.

I unlocked and removed the padlock that latched the door closed, and we stepped inside.

"Welcome to your Day-One accommodation!" I said cheerfully.

Ethan scanned the room briefly as if critiquing a piece of art.

"Looks like a dump, but yeah this should work," he said as he dropped his bag on the nearest bed.

"Cool. So what do you wanna do? Wanna grab some food, drinks, see some sights?

"Hmmmm, I choose option B….drinks!"

"What, no sight seeing?"

"Hey man, we'll get there! I just got off the plane and I need to unwind a little bit first," he said.

"Alright, I gotcha. Let's go then!"

"Hey hold on, I gotta drop a deuce first. Where's the shitter?"

"Ah, fine! It's down the hall. Take a right outside the door."

"Okay, be right back," he said, as he grabbed his travel guidebook and walked out of the room.

***

Having spent only a few days in Addis over the last few weeks, I didn't really know any of the local hotspots. However, I did know a decent place that I liked only a short walk toward the city center. We decided to leave the hotel and tackle the mean streets of Addis on foot.

"Man! How are we supposed to cross the street here? There's never a break in traffic," Ethan protested.

Walking down the street in Addis wasn't always as simple as it was in American cities. Even at stoplights, traffic still seemed to flow. So much so that sometimes it was safer to cross in the middle of the street rather than at the intersection.

"Well, there's a trick to it actually. It might sound a little backwards…but what you need to do is walk into the traffic and dodge each vehicle individually as you go across."

"Haha, yeah…okay. Let's see you try it then!"

"I know, I know. It goes against everything you've been taught, but trust me…that's how it's done."

"Fine. I'm waiting to see it then," he said in a challenging tone of voice.

"Alright, I hope you're taking notes."

Looking in the direction the oncoming traffic, I made my move into the street. With vehicles flowing toward me and all around me, I dodged each vehicle as I encountered it and eventually made my way to the other side in one seamless stride forward. The trick is actually to pace yourself so you don't end up standing in the middle of the road waiting for vehicles to pass.

"Oh okay, no problem!" Ethan yelled from across the road.

In a sudden jolt, he made a leap forward into the flow of traffic and proceeded to dodge each oncoming vehicle as they approached him. About half way into the street he had to pause for a moment and wait for a series of cars to pass by. All of a sudden, a heavy pocket of traffic forced him to make a quick sprint forward to the other side of the road where he got to the curb just before a motorcycle whizzed by.

"See, not bad," he said, looking obviously shaken.

"We'll work on it," I said smiling.

***

After a ten-minute walk, we arrived at a rooftop restaurant perched on top of a cement storefront. From the ground I could see the bright yellow cement fence that surrounded the terrace and the red plastic chairs and tables that were used to furnish it. In front of us, on the sidewalk was a painted-on sign with the words "Gaby's Restaurant" and a red arrow pointing up towards a set of stairs. We followed those stairs up and found a nice spot on the terrace overlooking the street. In the corner by the bar was a poster promoting St. George Beer that was being used to cover up a large crack in the wall. But to me, the poster was simply forecasting the beer that I was inevitably going to order.

"Wow, this place is crazy!" Ethan said while glaring down on the streets below.

"Yeah, not bad at all," I said, in my best "seasoned-backpacker" tone.

We sat on the balcony perched high above the chaos of Addis Ababa. From our red Coca-Cola sponsored table, chair and umbrella set, we had a great view of the streets below and welcomed shade from the sun. Two lukewarm St. George beers had made their way to our table to help jump start the afternoon, but having just arrived back in Addis, it probably wasn't required. I felt alive once again and ready to explore East Africa with my brother.

"So what's there to see here? What do people do when they come to Addis Ababa anyway?"

"I don't really think there's all that much to see here. The capital city itself isn't a huge tourist draw," I said confidently.

I had already been in Ethiopia for almost a month now and was more than happy to play the part of the seasoned traveler to my "fresh off the boat" younger brother. However when I initially arrived, I was probably even more lost and confused than he was.

I had booked my ticket on a whim after renting out my apartment and had very little time to educate myself on what I was in for. Even the decision of coming to Ethiopia was made quickly and hastily. I don't really know why I chose it. I guess I've always been drawn to it. My mother used to tell me as a child that "You need to finish all your vegetables because there are people starving in Ethiopia". I'm sure every American mother in the 1980's said that to her children, maybe in an attempt to foster appreciation for their luxuries. I guess it worked on me, but I'm not sure how my vegetable consumption helped a single starving farmer.

I had spent the first month here touring what is often called the "Historical Route". It consists of a loop around some of Ethiopia's more famous sites in the northern part of the country. Places like the ruins of Gondor, Lalibela and the Rock Hewn Churches of Tigray make this list. In fact, it has been one of the most exotic and interesting places I've ever seen.

"First time to Addis?" A voice said from behind us.

Surprised, I turned around to see the man who abruptly entered our conversation. He was thin, white and wore a scruffy brown beard. He had bloodshot eyes and looked very unimpressed by his current surroundings. One St. George beer sat on his table and was accompanied by a burning cigarette that laid in the standard-issue, Marlboro sponsored, white ashtray. To his right, he had a small notebook where he was jotting down notes in a leisurely manner.

"Well I was here a few weeks ago for a couple of days. Then spent some time up north in Axum, checking out the Stelae and the Arc of the Covenant," I said with a hint of sarcasm.

Little known to most people is that Ethiopia may be poor in resources but it's rich with historical significance. Ethiopia once was the seat of the great kingdoms of Axum and Gondor. Its countryside is scattered with remote churches carved right into its rocky cliffs. It is home to our oldest known hominid ancestor, Lucy. And it is where the Arc of the Covenant is said to reside. This last mention should be taken with a grain of salt since only a handful of monks are actually allowed to see it.

"I just came back to meet up with my younger brother. He just arrived today," I continued.

Expressionless, he looked at Ethan, "Welcome to Addis."

"Thanks," he replied as he sipped his beer.

It wasn't so easy to get Ethan here. After a lot of back-and-forth emails he had finally agreed to quit his job and meet me in Ethiopia. At first he was reluctant and didn't understand why, of all places, I had chosen Ethiopia. His idea of a vacation spot was a beach hut and a bottle of rum, which I admit, is hard to argue with. But Ethiopia I assured him, was one of the last untouched places left in the world. Backpackers were few and far between due to over exaggerated fears of war, famine and disease. In the end, he agreed to join me with no plan and nothing more than a plane ticket in and out of the region.

It wasn't really the sort of "good advice" an older brother should give to his younger brother, but it seemed like it made sense at the time. And after all, jobs come and go but the memory of a good trip will last forever. In matters like this, when you have the means to do something amazing, you should do it. It's more likely that you will regret your inactivity than your activity.

It's funny how in life our most important decisions, the ones that can change the course of our lives forever, are usually the ones where we have the least amount of information. To take a new job, to move to a new city, to end a relationship…with all these decisions come great uncertainty and create huge deviations in our respective paths. And the path not taken will always remain a mystery. Looking back on our lives, it's impossible for us to imagine any other reality than the one we are living, as our experiences have changed who we are. Maybe this is why we tend to say things like "everything happens for a reason" or "it was fate".

"So how 'bout you? Have you been here before?" I asked.

A smirk crept across his face as he took a drag from his cigarette, "Yeah, been here more times than I like to think about."

"For work?"

"You got it."

"Wow! What do you do that brings you to Ethiopia?" I said in a confused and jealous tone.

"I work for the BBC…. travel writer."

"Nice! You've got everyone's dream job."

"Trust me mate, the grass is always greener."

He appeared as if he had lost interest in seeing anything at all. He faced the restaurant with his back turned toward the street below as if he had spent a lifetime staring at those streets and there was nothing left to experience.

14

Emotionless, he took another drag of his cigarette, "My wife just had our first baby, but instead of being in London with my family I'm stuck here...choking on exhaust fumes and dreading tomorrow's long trip east. I spend half the year in some of the biggest shit holes in Africa. Ethiopia is actually a big step up compared to some of the other places I've gone. At least here they've got good food and an interesting culture. Try finding a decent meal in Chad!"

"Can't you get a gig in Europe or Asia?"

"Sometimes yes, but they're more competitive. Apparently people aren't breaking down the door to wander around rural Africa dodging militias and cholera outbreaks."

His apathy was actually intriguing. With most places I'd been to in the past, people had always wanted to be there. In some cases, they'd given up everything to get there. But here, something was different. There were almost no backpackers to be found in Ethiopia and little infrastructure to support them. The tourists that did come did it either via package tours or volunteer programs.

Our food had arrived and Ethan was sitting there quietly devouring his meal. His first day in Africa and he orders a plate of chicken Chow Mein and a side of fries. I tried to warn him that outside of Addis the selection might be limited to injera and goat meat, so I think he was attempting to get some variety while he could. Also, he had a long flight and wanted something familiar.

"So where are you guys headed? Back up north?"

"Actually we're not sure, but I imagine so. I really don't know much else about this part of Africa. I know at some point we'd like to make it to a beach, I was thinking we'd fly to Zanzibar in a week or so."

"Zanzibar is bollocks!" he said calmly but sternly.

"Bollocks?" I said, baffled at how someone could dislike this supposed tropical paradise I'd heard so much about.

"Unless you're looking to party with large Germans in small Speedos, skip it!"

"You're kidding! I heard it was absolutely beautiful!"

"Sure it's beautiful, but I can't imagine you came all the way to Africa to lay around in some resort. If you're looking for that, you might as well have gone to Hawaii. Plus, the Tanzanian government will charge you each $100 USD just for the visa. For my money, it's not worth it to spend a couple days on the beach."

It seemed like good information considering the source. However, Zanzibar was my selling point to Ethan to get him here in the first place. I turned to look at Ethan for his assessment of the situation. He looked up from his plate of noodles and simply shrugged.

"So what do you recommend?" Ethan said, addressing our new friend as if the conversation had finally gained his attention.

"Hawaii," the guy said, as if we'd made a bad choice in coming to Africa in the first place.

"Maybe some place on this continent?" I replied.

With a deep inhale of his cigarette he began to explain, "Just south of Mombasa there's a little beach town called Diani. Go there instead. It's a quick train ride from Nairobi and a popular spot for expats to decompress when they're not wasting away in central African shit holes," he paused for a moment only to take a breath. "But don't fly!" he insisted. "Flying is for package tourists.... it's for wankers! If you're headed to the beach, you might as well see Africa on your way there, because God knows real Africa doesn't spend its days sunbathing on a beach."

On this issue, he was passionate.

"Real Africa? What do you mean by real Africa?" Ethan said.

"The real Africa is in all the places that exist in between the places you've come here to see. It can't be found on a beach or on a Safari. You won't see it as part of a tour or on a volunteer program. The real Africa lives in between

16

those places. It's raw, uncomfortable, tiring and many times absolutely depressing. You can see the effects of it in the eyes of the NGO workers when once they've realized that all their efforts here have been for nothing...when they've realized that this is Africa and can't be made to be like Europe or America. Nor should it be!"

It was hard to tell if he was being real or just a little racist. Did he hate Africa or just understand it in a way most outsiders didn't? In my opinion, I still felt like I was in one of the most beautiful and exotic places on the planet. Whatever it was, something about him seemed authentic.

"But isn't that a bit of an over simplification? I mean, every country in Africa is different," Ethan said.

"Yes, of course they are all different. But they are also all very similar and as a result have very similar problems. Christ! We're talking about a continent whose countries have had their borders drawn arbitrarily by colonial powers! And those wankers didn't have a bloody clue what they were doing!"

I thought to myself, "Maybe he just hated everybody".

"Listen, if beaches are what you're after then do yourself a favor and take the road southbound out of Addis. Don't fly. You'll find beaches eventually along the Kenyan coast and in the process you'll actually understand what it means to be in Africa."

"What's so great about this road to Kenya?" I replied.

"Nothing. In fact it's one of the worst roads in Africa."

"Really? And we should take this road why?"

"Like I said, to see the real Africa. And if you do decide not to fly, it's really the only way out of the country. To the north, the Eritrean border is permanently closed. To the west is Sudan, and at the moment it's quite volatile. And to the east is Somalia, which is more or less a death sentence if you could even get into the country at all. Your only option out of Ethiopia, barring a flight, is by traveling south."

Ethan killed his beer and slammed it to the table making a satisfied "ahhh" sound. "I don't mind going south. It sounds like some badass shit, and I'm always down for some badass shit! Hey, you got a smoke?"

I pushed the pack of Ethiopian cigarettes in his direction, silently still pondering our options.

"So how do we get there?" I asked.

"Just make your way to the Addis central bus station on the morning you want to leave…7AM or so. As you know, there's no such thing as reservations here. Just show up and get on," he replied as if he was starting to warm up to us.

Nodding in agreement, I turned to Ethan, "So you don't mind skipping the north, the ancient city of Lalibela, the Stella of Axum, the Arc of the Covenant? Northern Ethiopia has some of the most amazing sites in the world."

"Screw it man! Leave the Stella for the package tourists and the Arc for Indiana Jones. The south sounds like the real adventure, not to mention it's in the direction of the beach," he said smiling.

Ethan was a chronic beach bum. I blame its association to beer and bikinis.

"Ahh, I see your real motivation here. But I'd hardly classify northern Ethiopia as 'overly touristy'. I don't think I saw more than a handful of foreigners the whole time I was up there."

"And," he interrupted, "I just got to Africa today so I'm not about to start this trip off by acting like a wanker," purposely incorporating a new word into his vocabulary.

"Well, I guess we're going south then," I said definitively.

Despite how much I loved my time in northern Ethiopia, I had no real drive to get back so soon.

"Sounds good," Ethan responded with the excitement that a decision had been made.

He burst up from the plastic red table and said, "Two more beers….or three?" looking at our new friend.

"Oh, no more for me mate. I need to get back to my hotel and get some sleep. I'm not as young or as excited as you two."

"Okay, fair enough," Ethan said as he walked toward the bar and ordered two more beers.

"So are you guys planning on sitting here all day and getting pissed?"

"No, I don't think so…at least I hope not," I said smiling. "I thought we'd head over to the Mercado in a bit."

"Well, leave your valuables in your hotel room," he replied nonchalantly.

The Addis Mercado is the central market of the city and is infamous for pickpockets and thieves but still well worth a visit.

He ashed his cigarette, tossed a wad of Ethiopian Bur on the table as he got up to leave.

The Bur is the national currency of Ethiopia. It usually takes the form of dirty ripped up paper bills and comes in a variety of colors based on denomination. Its low exchange rate to the dollar makes it feel like "play money" to most foreigners. The goal is to try to fight this perception in order to prevent over spending.

"What were your boys' names again?" he said before leaving.

"Dean…and that's Ethan. And you?"

"William."

"Nice to meet you. Maybe we'll see you around."

"Well if you hang around East Africa long enough, you will," he said with his first smile of the entire conversation, and walked away.

Moments later Ethan returned with two ice-cold St. George's and huge smile on his face.

"Look, I got cold ones!" he said, as if he'd just accomplished something amazing.

In fact, he did. Electricity was sporadic in Ethiopia, even in the capital. As a result, beer was often drunk warm.

Ethan was quickly catching on to the fact that some basic luxuries might be significantly less abundant here. It didn't seem to faze him in the slightest though. He had a way of ignoring the details of a situation and focusing on the task at hand. In this case, it was acquiring beer for a mid-afternoon buzz.

"Beautiful. Cheers!"

"Cheers…to Africa!" Ethan said in a cheesy tone.

"Oh shut up! Just drink your beer," I replied smiling.

CHAPTER 3
ONE NIGHT IN ADDIS

Away from our rooftop restaurant, we found ourselves amidst the hustle and bustle of Addis Ababa. With only a vague idea of where to go, we made our way west towards the Mercado. As we walked, we were perhaps the two most popular people on the street. Every step of the way we received stares, hellos, waves and pressure from taxi drivers to take a ride. Sidewalks were non-existent most of the way so we were forced to navigate the dusty streets while dodging pedestrians, taxis, open sewer gates and ever so common white mini-buses, otherwise known as matatus.

Our destination, the Addis Mercado, is the largest open-air market in all of Africa and nearly everything imaginable passes within its perimeter. It is a messy, chaotic labyrinth of vendors selling everything from household goods, to food, to cloths. From what I knew, it was easy to locate but difficult to navigate.

"Hey! Let's stop here for a second. I need to get a water," I said.

"Alright," Ethan stopped behind me and looked out onto the street.

The hot Ethiopian sun was beating down on me as I walked up to a corner store selling one-liter bottles of water. The store itself couldn't have been more than five by five feet wide and combined with all the other merchandise; the owner could barely fit inside.

21

"One water please."

"Five Birr," the man said from behind the counter.

The official language of Ethiopia is "Amharic" and nobody anywhere else in the world speaks it. So English is pretty common out of necessity. This was good news for us.

I paid the man, grabbed my water and turned around to see Ethan speaking with two local guys. They couldn't have been much older than we were.

"Fuck," I said under my breath, immediately thinking that they were working on a plan to rip him off.

It's not that I don't have faith in people; it's just that it's hard to trust people who randomly approach you on a street corner and engage in conversation. In my experience, the only people who do that are the ones that want something from you. Usually it's an accurate assumption.

Ethan had bummed them each a cigarette and they looked as if they were all enjoying each other's company over a smoke. This just meant that we had to put up with them until they made their pitch.

"Hey, what's up!" I said, as I approached them.

"Hey man," Ethan responded.

Immediately they acknowledged my arrival, "Hello," each of them said as we shook hands.

"Hi! How are you guys?" I responded in my happiest tone.

"Very good. Are you also from America?"

"Yup, we both live in California but originally from North Dakota."

I immediately felt stupid for telling him that we were originally from North Dakota, like he had any idea where that was. Most Americans don't even know where it is let alone some kid on the other side of the planet.

Ethan and I had grown up in North Dakota and had lived there up until the age of 18. It was only a matter of time until each of us had to escape the brutally cold winters. Myself, being the oldest left first and headed east to Minnesota where I earned a degree in business. Ethan, being slightly more rebellious took a year off and then decided to move to Colorado to pursue school and a career as a ski bum.

Once our schooling was finished we both somehow ended up in California, although not at the same time nor in the same place. I was living the corporate life in San Francisco while Ethan worked part-time as an assistant manager at a popular bar on Pacific Beach in San Diego. As it turned out, we were just a couple of cliché country boys trying to live the California dream.

We began to exchange the standard niceties that all tourists, travelers and locals will eventually ask one another. Where are you from? Where have you been? How long are you traveling for? …All the standard "get to know you" questions.

After a few moments of group conversation, I made the move to break away. My hope was to slip out gracefully and not look like a complete jackass.

"Well, alright guys. We're going to take a walk around the Mercado for a bit. Have a good one!" I said as we slowly started to walk away.

Sure enough, they began to follow.

"Oh, that's great! We can show you around for a while if you don't mind?"

"Sure, let's go," Ethan said, without giving me a chance to say otherwise.

And like that, we had a tail. Why did Ethan always have to be so friendly? Damn him!

"There are many interesting things to buy in the Mercado, but be very careful. There are many bad people who will try to take your money here!" one of them warned us.

I'd done this a million times before…. played the role of nice and naive tourist while constantly monitoring every move they made and every place they took us. You have to be cautious when you're abroad. Everywhere you go, you're a target. Yet I can't blame them; I'd do the same thing if I were in their shoes.

"So what are your guys' names?" Ethan said.

"I am Staven and this is Abdi," one of them said.

"Nice to meet you both," Ethan replied.

"Yes, follow me. I can show you the interesting things in the Mercado," said Staven.

It wasn't long before we reached the edge of the Mercado. At the end of the road we could see it in front of us, a dense mass of humanity seething with commerce. Like an open plain leading up to a dense forest, there was no uncertainty as to where it began.

"Come. We can see the shops," said Staven.

The four of us successfully managed to "Frogger" ourselves across the heavy traffic without a single man down. Once on the other side we cautiously stepped into the madness of the Mercado. Staven and Abdi walked in front leading us through the tiny winding alleyways while pointing out the various aspects of the market that made it unique.

On every side of us were shopkeepers selling all types of products. Some new some recycled. Some local, some shipped from across the world. Some of the goods were familiar like lawn chairs and pots and pans. Others were strange to see like old boom boxes and wicker baskets over flowing with exotic spices. The walkways became smaller as we hiked deeper into the heart of the commerce and with every step we took; more eyes began to focus on us. It appeared that we had entered a part of the Mercado that few foreigners visit, thanks to our new "friends".

Staven explained to us that within the madness there was an order that lay beneath the surface. Despite the chaotic appearance, the market was arranged into sections, each one focusing on a specific product or category. Food stuffs, electronics, aluminum, spices, plastics…all organized into their own sections.

After about 15 minutes into the Mercado we had reached an obstacle in our path. Before us flowed a slow moving river of sewage at the bottom of a six-foot deep ravine surrounded by trash on all sides. With only a pair of two by eight inch boards laid across each bank for a makeshift walking bridge, people crossed effortlessly from side to side. One wrong step and it suddenly became a horrible afternoon. Staven and Abdi crossed along with everyone else without a second thought, while Ethan and I needed a minute to assess the situation.

"Holy shit!" Ethan's eyes grew large. "What the hell is this?"

"This, my friend, is a river of shit."

"You're not kidding."

We both paused for a moment staring at our only option across. It was either cross the wobbly 16-inch bridge or turn around and admit right then and there that we were no match for even the simplest Ethiopian obstacle. With dozens of eyes staring at us, our pride was now on the line. There was no other choice. With a sudden acceptance, Ethan simply shrugged his shoulders and walked across the bridge. In many ways he was more daring than I was, and this time it showed.

"Come on man, it's easy. Get over here!" he shouted from the safe side.

Being the last man standing, I had no other alternative but to cross the bridge. As I cautiously made my way forward, the two wooden planks wobbled uncomfortably beneath my feet. The six feet of distance across felt like twice that. With hands stretched out like a gymnast, I slowly started on my way to the other side. With each foot carefully placed in front of the other, I noticed out of the corner of my eye that there were now people on both sides waiting for me to get off the bridge. The pressure didn't help the situation. For a second as I focused on the bystanders instead of the wobbly planks, I began to feel myself leaning too much to my right. It was too late. I couldn't catch my balance. In one swift move I jumped from the plank with my left foot and landed on the other side. With a deep exhale; I stood there relieved that I didn't fall into the river of shit below.

Despite my inner turmoil no one else seemed to notice; after all, it was only a six-foot crossing. Within seconds a woman with a basket on her head nudged me aside and crossed the bridge without the slightest inconvenience.

As if he had no idea why I was taking so long, Staven simply said, "Come, this way!"

The dynamic between our two new friends was slowly becoming clear. Staven was the talkative one, and the obvious leader. He had an aura of urgency about him, something that made his movements seem slightly aggressive. Abdi, on the other hand, rarely said a word and was perfectly content being led. He seemed to be an observer of life, satisfied with simply keeping to himself the things that transpired in his mind. If they weren't so different they would have never gotten along so well.

We turned a corner to reach the end of an alleyway. Before us, it opened up to a large expanse where hundreds of people worked diligently in chaotic harmony. This was the "recycling center" of the Mercado.

"My friends, this is where we make old things new," said Staven.

"Old things new?' Ethan replied.

"Yes, unlike in your country we recycle everything we can. What you call trash, to us can still have good use."

There, in the open expanse of the Mercado was the most unique aspect of any market I had seen anywhere. It was where trash came to be reborn. There were sections where people sat diligently pounding bent rebar straight again. Women sat on crates in the dirt in long rows viciously scrubbing old pots and pans to a like-new shimmer. Old electronics like 1980's style Boom Boxes were carefully being repaired and old plastic bottles were rounded up for re-use. For people who have so little everything that can be reused, is reused. Our wasteful culture back home would be wise to take notes.

Despite the uniqueness of the area, we made our way through it fairly quickly. There was so much chaos occurring all around us that it felt odd to be standing in the way of it all. When we reached the edge of the Mercado it was obvious that the commerce jungle had ended abruptly. From where we stood, the rest of Addis began again.

"My friends, that was the Mercado. As you can see it is quite large!" said Staven.

"Pretty cool, should we grab a drink?" Ethan said as he surveyed the streets in front of him.

"Damn dude! It's like 4PM," I replied.

Ethan wasn't someone who was really interested in traveling in the traditional sense. He liked to go to new places but when he got somewhere he had little motivation to see anything. He was definitely one of those travelers you'd see wasting away days not leaving the hostel, the whole while meeting every single traveler in his path. In this case however, he wasn't completely on his own.

As soon as Staven heard Ethan's request for beer he perked up, "You want to drink? I will show you where we can go! Come this way."

Despite our better judgment, we aimlessly followed them towards the establishment of their choice. I guess they didn't come off as very threatening. Both Staven and Abdi were short and thin in typical Ethiopian fashion and each of them wore a t-shirt and a pair of faded blue jeans. Staven sported the added accessory of a backwards baseball cap with the word "Okley" stitched onto the front. In African street markets it was not uncommon to find knockoff merchandise posing as the real thing by slightly changing the spelling of a popular brand name. In this case the original word would have read "Oakley".

"How many days do you stay in Addis?" Staven asked.

"We're taking off tomorrow," Ethan replied.

"And where will you go?"

"South. To Kenya, I guess," Ethan said, unsure of himself.

"How will you get there?"

"By bus I think. Is there another way?"

"Yes, of course! You don't want to take the local bus. It is very slow. First I will take you to my friend. He has a matatu that can take you south tomorrow morning."

In Africa, the matatu is the ever-so-common white mini-van that has evolved into the preferred mode of transportation for most people. They operate like a shared taxi. Matatus are usually considered slightly more comfortable and quite a bit faster than busses. The "faster" part I can agree with but to say that they are "comfortable" is a stretch of the imagination.

"That's okay," I interjected. "We don't want to buy our tickets in advance. We'll just get them at the bus station tomorrow. Thanks though."

There was no way I was going to hand over any cash to some kids on the street for a "ticket" that was good for the next day.

"No, you don't pay now. Pay tomorrow when he picks you up. You pay the driver," Staven said smiling.

I nodded at Ethan, "Well, that might be okay then."

Before stopping at the bar we made our way to a small house not far from where the Mercado was. It was built in a similar fashion to most homes in the area; with a concrete structure, a metal roof and a patchy coat of paint…green in this case. The door was propped open and hanging off of one hinge. Inside, I could only see a woman watching an old TV in the front room of the house.

"What is your hotel?" Staven asked.

"Ahhh, Wutma Hotel," I said, trying to remember the name.

"Okay, wait here," Staven instructed as he jolted across the street toward the house.

With time to kill, Ethan, Abdi and myself sat on a set of concrete steps near a juice vendor on the opposite side of the road while Staven took care of our transportation plans. As we waited, we each enjoyed one of Ethiopia's famous "Spris" smoothies while positioning ourselves in the shade provided by concrete building towering behind us.

For whatever reason, and quite unexpectedly, Ethiopia has somehow managed to master the art of producing fresh fruit smoothies. Their most unique creation is something called a "Spris" which has three separate layers of blended mango, papaya and avocado. The avocado has sugar added to it, so despite what you might assume, tastes great in a smoothie form. It's usually served cold and in a glass mug with a straw.

"So where are you from?" I asked Abdi, trying to make conversation.

"I am from Wollo Provence, in the north. It is not far."

"Oh I see. I may have traveled near there a few weeks ago. Is it near Tigray?"

"Yes, close."

There was a short pause, as it seemed like he had little interest in chatting. He was a man of few words, but I didn't let that stop me.

"So why did you decide to come to Addis?"

"I left with my family when I was very young. The rain stopped coming, so the crops did not grow. My father moved us here to find work, but it is not easy," he said stoically.

"Oh wow. And what do you do for work here?" I asked.

"I do whatever I can."

Just then Staven came bolting across the street and interrupted my progress in getting to know Abdi.

"Okay, he will meet you outside your hotel at 3AM tomorrow morning. Good?"

"Holy hell!" Ethan said. "3am?!"

"And how much is that?" I said.

"Only 500 Birr each. You can pay tomorrow."

It actually wasn't a bad price so we agreed despite the ridiculous hour that we were scheduled to leave. Worst-case scenario, these guys murder us shortly after picking us up. However, a more probable scenario was that they just don't show up, in which case we go back to sleep and hop on a bus later in the day. We were ready to make that bet. With our plans in order, we were now free to relax and enjoy the rest of our time in Addis, as limited as it was.

"Okay, now we drink!" exclaimed Staven, like a man on a mission.

He led and we followed. And as we followed, we made our way down the main thoroughfares of Addis slowly approaching the neighborhoods in the outer areas. The roads changed from wide lanes with partial sidewalks to narrow lanes made of dirt and gravel. On the sides of the road, the partial sidewalks slowly morphed into ditches that collected rainwater and trash. The further away we progressed from the city center, the more people began to stare as we passed by. We were approaching areas that saw few foreigners. As the dirt roads began to change into alleyways, I began struggling to keep my sense of direction. Winding and turning, dodging kids on bikes and potholes...we kept moving until all of a sudden, we stopped.

There, to the left of us was a small gap about four feet wide between two cement houses, both of which appeared to be abandoned. It was nearly pitch black now as we were well beyond the parts of town that had streetlights. As we walked single file into the space between the two houses, we could hear the noise increase as we approached. We followed Staven and Abdi through an opening and down a set of cement stairs that led into a small dimly lit room. At its entrance, an overweight woman was sitting in a chair guarding the door. It appeared as if she knew Staven and immediately granted us passage by simply exchanging a few words and nodding in his direction.

Through the smoke and haze we could barely make out

the faces looking back at us but it seemed as if many of them were under 18 years old. Before we had arrived they were all drinking and speaking loudly in Amharic, but nearly instantaneously the conversation stopped and all eyes focused on us.

Staven began to speak to a few of them in Amharic and smiles slowly began to creep across their faces. Within moments, the drinking continued and the gathering was back to its original intensity. While he spoke the women at the door had turned around and began to fill up four small glasses with a clear vodka-like drink. She passed them to Staven.

"Here!" he said. "This is arak."

"Arak?" I said confused. "What is it?"

"Alcohol," he said as if he was speaking to a child. "It will be 20 Birr."

We paid, of course. It was simply unspoken that we would pay for every cost incurred that evening. After all, we made more in a day than they made in a month and things were cheap.... really cheap.

Without hesitation Staven and Abdi began to drink, then Ethan, then me. Forcing a look of disgust into one of acceptance, I slowly choked down my beverage. It burned like any liquor but with a distinct flavor of rubbing alcohol. It turned out that it was a standard homemade rice wine concoction. Here they call it "arak", in other regions "roxy", but in most places it's just referred to as "rice wine". I've even seen it come in little plastic bags while in some countries. But let me tell you, when you start drinking liquor out of a little plastic bag, you know that you've reached a new stage in life.

With any homemade rice wine I knew there were inherent risks involved, but sometimes you just end up putting trust in people, smart or not. A few years back I had been traveling in Cambodia when a batch of bad rice wine had killed off an entire village of men. The problem is that there's no regulation on this stuff, so it's up to the guy brewing it in his bathtub to not add anything deadly to the mix. Luckily for us, this was a good batch.

As we drank we made small talk with those who were able to work up the nerve to mingle with us. And the more we drank the more the overweight lady in the corner would refill our cups. As I looked around the cramped and dingy room, I realized that even on the other side of the world in a place so far removed, kids are all the same. Whether they live here in Ethiopia, North Dakota or California, kids everywhere are just trying to party.

It didn't take long before our group got anxious and it was time for us to make our way to our next destination. We said our goodbyes, paid our bill and thanked them for their hospitality. At this point the sun was beginning to go down and we were starting to feel good. We made our way back to the alley outside of the two abandoned-looking houses and began our walk back towards town.

"So now what?" said Ethan, clearly ready for the evening to get into full swing.

Ethan was an instigator. He was that guy who always kept the party going or was pushing for the next one to start. Every crew needed an "Ethan".

Staven chimed in, "We can do anything! We have bars, whore houses, chat houses. There are many things in Addis. What do you like?"

It was becoming clear that Ethan and Staven were feeding off each other's energy. And to top it off, their motivations complimented each other. Ethan was looking for a good time, which Staven could provide and Staven was looking for a free night out, which Ethan was more than willing to cover. They were unstoppable.

"Chat house? What's that?" Ethan said.

"It is a place where people go to chew chat together…like a bar or a restaurant but for chat," Staven explained.

"And what the hell is chat? He said as he looked at me to see if I knew what this stuff was.

"Oh sorry," I said. "It's local plant that people chew to get high. It's a stimulant but it takes a while to kick in. It doesn't mess you up but it does wake you up!"

"So it's like coke?"

"Eh, not really. I'd say it falls somewhere in between cocaine and coffee...but it's legal here."

"Oh, we've got to try this!" he said with excitement. "Have you tried it before?"

"Yeah, a few times. It's alright," I said, as if I was a veteran chat chewer.

"Well, how to we find it?" Ethan exclaimed.

"You want chat? We can get that. Come! My friend will sell to us," said Staven.

Staven had a friend for everything.

As we walked in the direction of Staven's "chat guy" we made our way out of the small alleys and dirt roads and onto an area closer to the city center. We were still on the peripheral but now much closer. From where we stood in the darkness, I could see the glow of Addis in the distance. So at least I had a general direction of how to get back if needed.

The streets were still dark without public lighting and the only light that filled the air came from small fires or individual light bulbs hanging from private residences. People walked through the darkness chatting as stray dogs scrounged for food in the stillness. It was hard to picture a chat house in a place like this but what did I really know. This was a local area.

"You will like chat," Staven assured Ethan. "It is very nice for staying awake and fucking a long time!...hahaha!"

Awkwardly, Ethan just looked at him and smiled, "Haha, okay."

Within a few moments we had reached our destination. It was a rickety looking house with the front door closed. Beams of light broke through the cracks in the door, illuminating the street in front of us. With a knock and a push, Staven opened the door and a bright neon light shined down on us from the open entrance of the chat house. We walked in single file.

The room was painted bright pink with eight chairs positioned in a semi-circle and a small blue table set in the middle. As we entered the room I could see we were in the right place. There were already three guys sitting there sharing a bushel of chat. They glared at us with beady eyes and eerie smiles as they continued to chew chat and smoke cigarettes. The smoke in the air was thick and ventilation was non-existent.

"Please sit. I will speak with the manager," Staven instructed as he walked off.

We pulled up three chairs in a row across from the first three chat-chewers in the semicircle. Abdi sat closest to them. For a moment we sat in silence as we waited for Staven to return. The guys across from us smiled with ever more welcoming gestures as Abdi began to make small talk in Amharic. Perhaps he was vouching for us.

I could tell that Abdi was a quiet yet friendly guy. He had a slightly nerdy or analytical vibe about him. If he had been born in the states I could see him being a software developer in Silicon Valley. He reminded me a lot of the people I used to work with in that area.

It wasn't long before Staven returned with two bushels of chat, each in a black plastic bag and two glass bottles of Coca-Cola. He shut the door behind him and sat down in one of the vacant chairs.

"Okay my friends!" he said in excitement as he placed the bushels on the blue table and pulled the first one out of the black plastic bag.

He and Abdi began to dig into the first bushel as if they couldn't wait. Ethan and I sat watching cautiously. Staven carefully pulled the tips off each of the leaves and proceeded to roll them into a tiny ball. He handed the first ball to Ethan.

"Here, try this," he said.

"So how do I do this exactly?" Ethan replied in

amusement.

"Just take these leaves and chew them. You can swallow the juice. If the taste is too bad for you, you can take some Coke," he said as he handed Ethan the first bottle of Coke anticipating a negative reaction from the chat.

"Some people like to eat the whole leaf and the stem, but they are savages! We only eat the tips of the leaves because they are the best!

Staven then glanced at me, "You have had chat before, yes?"

"Sure. I've tried it a few times since I've been here," I said.

"Excellent! Please, help yourself," he said with a smile.

As we sat there chewing our chat our heart rates began to speed up, our pupils dilated and the room slowly began to get more and more friendly and vibrant. I could feel my mouth getting dry but I was slowly getting used to the taste of the bitter chat leaves. Still, my Coca-Cola consumption remained constant. The room was filling with cigarette smoke as the chat-induced adrenaline surged through us. Our group had merged with the one next to us, although Abdi sat in the corner not saying much as usual.

Whenever we didn't chew the chat fast enough, Staven would roll us a little ball of leaves and give it to Ethan or me. It was hard to keep up and my cheeks began to become full of green leaves. The bottles of Coke made their way around the room but Ethan and I drank the majority, as we were new to the harsh taste of the leaves.

As the minutes passed and the first bushel made way for the second, we kept chewing and kept on talking. But the second bushel went faster than the first and soon, through the smoke and conversation, it was evident that our stash was nearly depleted. Energized and ready to hit the town, we all agreed that it was time to head to the bar. Before we could leave, however, we had to pay our bill. Again, this fell on us. And I knew from experience that when you don't get the price up front, you end up paying for it in the end. Sure enough, that is exactly what happened.

After a few moments of sitting there chat-less, a small boy approached us with a yellow post-it note sized piece of paper and handed it to Staven. He looked at it and immediately came over to explain it to me.

"The price is 700 Birr, 300 for each bushel of chat and 100 for the Cokes," he said cautiously as if he was expecting some push back from me.

"Ohh okay. That should be no problem," I said.

He was in luck. I was feeling generous from the chat and actually I was expecting it to be higher. The total cost came to around $30 USD, much more expensive than it should have been but nothing that would break the bank.

Once paid up, we were free to leave and from the comfort of our cozy little chat den we made our way into the dark desolate side streets of Addis Ababa toward the more lively area of the Piazza. This, the historical Italian area, was now known mostly for pickpockets, hookers, drinking and all types of general debauchery.

Our destination turned out to be a club at the center of the Piazza's madness. It was a black, non-descript building with two large Bob Marley murals on either side of the entrance. Ethiopians had a bit of a national obsession with Bob Marley due to the fact that they are so closely tied to the Rastafarian religion that sprung out of Jamaica.

In the 1930's, individuals in Jamaica began to identify the Ethiopian emperor, Haile Selassie as the returned messiah prophesied in the bible. It was at this time that the Rastafarian religion was born. It was thought that he would usher in a golden age of prosperity into the world and is essentially the Rasta equivalent to Jesus or Mohammad. Somewhere along the line pot smoking and reggae music got thrown in the mix, a nice addition to any religion.

In front of the club, the entrance was surrounded by

people talking, drinking, smoking and just generally waiting to get inside. They had organized themselves in a cluster, rather than a single file line in hopes of being closest to the door. Being the only foreign faces in the crowd, we were immediately approached and let in. I guess they wanted to diversify their demographics or maybe they just assumed we would spend a lot on drinks. Regardless, our tiny group walked in right past the bouncer.

Inside it looked like any club that you might find back in the States. Near the entrance there were tall round tables scattered around a lounge-like area and in the back there was a dance floor with a bar set off to the right. The dance floor consisted mainly of women dancing with each other in a circle while apprehensive men stood around the periphery watching and gaining liquid courage as they plotted their moves. Another perfect example of how some things are just the same everywhere. The music being played was familiar as well. Over the stereo I could recognize the raspy "Okay!" of Lil John blaring out from the speakers. This could have been any club anywhere in the world.

Almost immediately we were able to find a table near the dance floor. It was close enough to people-watch but not so close where we would feel obligated to dance. We ordered a round of beers but unfortunately they didn't want our money until the end. Somewhere in the back of my mind my better judgment knew this would end up biting us in the ass but the alcohol in my system allowed me to easily ignore that feeling. Like all clubs, it was too loud to talk to each other, so like any group of guys we stood around our table and drank. As we drank, we watched. And as we watched, we became noticed.

From across the room came two of the most beautiful girls in the club…perhaps the world. They made a beeline to Ethan and me without giving a second look to Staven or Abdi. Normally this might make a couple of guys feel pretty good about themselves, having so easily "out competed" two others. But here in this club, we stood out for another very obvious reason. These girls didn't like us. They didn't have a thing for white boys. The only color on their mind was "green". In a country where people make so little, anything, even getting a free drink, is time well spent.

So time passed, we flirted, and the drinks came and went. All the while we knew that they were only there for the drinks that would inevitably end up being added to our tab. But how do you walk away from, not one, but two girls who look like Beyoncé? If there's a way, I'd love to hear it.

In the end, our table may have had a drink for every person but we still lacked a girl for every man. As a result, it wasn't long before the smiles on Ethan's and my face had an adverse effect on the already discontented disposition of our fellow drinking buddies, who had already felt as if life had given them the short end of the stick. In a sudden burst, Staven pushed over his nearly full beer and stormed out towards the door. Abdi of course followed after him.

As if breaking us from a trance, Ethan and I looked up and proceeded to run out to see what had happened. As we attempted to exit the club the bouncers stopped us at the doorway insisting that we pay our bill immediately, which despite the unusually high price tag, we did promptly. From the entrance, Staven could see Ethan paying for all the drinks without even flinching at the price as he walked toward the door. This made him hysterical.

From outside the club on the sidewalk, he stared screaming, "See you can have everything, and we have nothing! You get the girls inside, we get no girls! You pay for the drinks without any cares! And what do we have?...only shit!"

"Staven, I'm sorry man! We all know they only wanted the free drinks," Ethan said, trying to talk him down.

"I don't care! At least you have money! Never in my

life can I do that, but you live like kings. Are you better than us? I don't think so, and yet you have everything!"

In a furry, Staven pushed me in the chest and I fell into the bouncer at the door. He turned around, broke through the crowd and made a U-turn down an alley. After struggling to get up, I ran around the corner after him and stopped where the alley met the street. There I stood with Ethan, watching him walk away into the darkness of the Piazza. Abdi again, followed after him.

Within moments they had completely disappeared into the night and with as much ease as they had approached us, they had left. Now alone and in a state of shock we needed to either keep drinking or make our way home. With a heavy feeling of guilt we chose to go home, which, luckily for us was not far off.

Drunk and slightly stunned by what had occurred, it was official that our first night in Addis had come to an abrupt end. As Ethan and I made our way out through the dark streets of the Piazza to our hotel on the outskirts of the neighborhood, we could feel the silence of the city. There were no more partygoers, taxis or street vendors and nothing to do but sleep. Aside from the occasional stray dog roaming alone in the night, it was only the two of us and the thought of our long journey ahead.

CHAPTER 4
LEAVING ADDIS ABABA

"How ya feelin?"

"Like shit," Ethan responded while pulling out a cigarette.

As he lit it I could see the spark cast a shadow down the desolate Ethiopian road. A puff of smoke and it was dark again.

There we sat in the dark, on the side of the road staring into the blackness beneath the brothel that served as our hotel the night before. The overwhelming silence provided a strangely peaceful feeling despite the ominous backdrop. From the distance we could see a man stumbling across the road.

"Probably just a drunk," I said to Ethan

"Mmm hmm," he said in agreement as he stared off into space.

Periodically a car or van would drive by and we'd perk our heads up in anticipation, each time lowering them slowly in disappointment. We were waiting for our ride out of town…or were we? It was early and starting to look like it was time to give up.

"If they don't show up, I'm walking right back into that whore house and going back to sleep!" I said in frustration.

"Mmm hmm," Ethan said in response.

Ethan didn't talk much when he was tired, and we were practically sleepwalking.

From out of nowhere and with a sudden break in the

silence, came a pair of glowing headlights in the distance. Through the beams of the headlights, a cloud of dust and dirt could be seen as a vehicle barreled down the dirt road towards us. Was this our ride? Did the guys from last night actually come through?

I stood up and busted out my standard "taxi cab wave" in an attempt to make our presence known in the off chance that our ride had indeed arrived. Ethan, unconvinced and unimpressed made no movements and displayed no emotion. As the van came closer my anticipation raised until…sure enough…it passed right by us spewing dust in my face.

I knew we were just waiting for a ride, but my heart sank a bit. I think my lack of sleep had made me emotional. Then all of a sudden, fifty feet or so in front of us, the white van made a sudden stop and with grinding gears began a slow reversal toward us. It was a sudden but beautiful disruption to the silence of the night.

With a burst, I yelled out to Ethan, "Dude! Our ride's here!"

"Oh hell yeah," he murmured, as if awaking from a deep sleep.

With our bags draped across our right shoulders and that "staring into the sun" look, we both grabbed our things and walked cautiously toward the dimly lit, barely perceivable, dusty, white van on the opposite side of the road.

"Hello," I said as we approached the driver's rolled down window.

"Hello. You are for Dila?" he asked as he exhaled a puff of smoke from his cigarette.

"Yes, I guess so," I said, with the biggest smile I could muster. "South to Kenya."

Dila wasn't actually part of our plan but it was the closest big town on the road south. So at least we'd be moving in the right direction.

"Okay, come!" he said as he gestured with a head nod

to the sliding door on the opposite side.

I opened the door and there were three pairs of bright white eyes staring back at me in what seemed like a mix of surprise and exhaustion. It was 3AM and nobody wanted to be awake. A fourth person was sitting up in the middle row with his head leaning on the window, fast asleep. He had it all figured out.

As I stepped in, Ethan followed and we made our way to the back corner of the van as to not get in anyone's way. After all, I had no idea how this process was supposed to work. Should we pay now or on arrival? Did we make bathroom breaks or lunch stops? How long was this trip? These were all questions that most people would have tried to find answers to prior to getting into a stranger's van in the middle of the night. It appeared we did things a little differently. Instantly the sliding door slammed shut and we took off into the night with our bags propped up on our laps.

On our way out of the city, we would occasionally pick up additional passengers every few miles, which resulted in an ever increasingly cramped travel situation. At every pickup, the arriving passenger would look back at the two white boys in the corner with a look of silent surprise or at most a simple smile and a few words in Amharic to the other riders.

Once the van was at maximum capacity and no more passengers could fit inside, we picked up another two people who somehow managed to eke out a spot on the floor and center console. The big luggage, including our bags, was now tied to the roof of the van while the smaller and more delicate items were kept inside. By the time we left the Addis sprawl, I was crammed up against the window and Ethan crammed up against me. On his right was a colorfully dressed, overweight African woman, and on his lap was a steel cage, and in that cage was a rooster. He seemed to take it well enough.

As we drove off into the night, the city of Addis Abba

slowly began to change from the urban jungle of the city center, to the stereotypical slums that encircled most large African cities, to the farms that dotted the rural landscape. Buildings became houses then houses made way for shacks with tin roofs, until mud or wooden huts replaced the shacks.

With no more passengers to pick up, the van took on a soothing aura as our team of misfits rolled off into the Ethiopian countryside. Outside, there was no light to see anything aside from the occasional stray dog on the side of the road that got caught in the beam of our headlights. It was still pitch black out and everyone was too tired to speak. Once away from any traffic, the rhythm of the rolling van put us all to sleep. Despite the close situation, we all managed to drift off…even the rooster.

CHAPTER 5
THE ENVELOPE

I awoke to the sun creeping up from the horizon and beads of sweat dripping down from my forehead. It couldn't have been later than 8AM and it was already getting hot. Ethan was awake next to me with his headphones in listening to music. I could hear the muffled sound of screeching guitars blaring out of his ear buds. After looking around the van I noticed that everyone else was awake…even the rooster.

Finally in the light of day, the Ethiopian countryside began to come alive as we passed the small towns, villages and subsistence farmers that make up the heart of the country. As we rushed across the dusty, dry road heading south, we could see daily life unfolding as farmers plowed fields using traditional oxen and plows, women tended to crops and children played with toys built from whatever limited materials they could scrounge up. The farms were as basic as they could possibly be, a field with a shack and no irrigation systems in sight. This was the life of a rural Ethiopian farmer. With each village or farm we passed, the onlookers would stop whatever they were doing and wave at us as if they had a friend inside.

As we progressed south, the hills of the north gave way to an immense valley that stretched for miles in every direction. This was the beginning of the Great Rift Valley of East Africa where the oldest humanoid remains were once found and where the African continent is literally being pulled apart in opposite directions by plate tectonics. The result of which are the flat, sun scorched plains that now serve as home to villagers who seem to live a life isolated from the rest of mainstream society. For better or worse, time moves slower here, as if the advances of the outside world left it behind.

I looked over at Ethan and he seemed to be pretty content now that he was able to lose himself in his music. He just sat nodding his head as he looked out at the countryside. Not a bad plan, but having seen a lot of Ethiopia over the last month I had a different idea in mind.

Before I left, my dad had given me a series of short stories that he had written about my grandfather, who had died just a few months earlier. His death was exceptionally impactful as he had always been the glue that held our family together. So when he died, it forced everyone to take a step back and really evaluate how they would move forward in a world without him.

My dad had written these stories; perhaps as a way of grieving or as a way to solidify my grandfather's legacy. For me, I hoped they might shed some light on to who he truly was, at a time when I was too young to really know him.

I received this packet of stories about a week before my departure but hadn't had a chance to read them until now. For some reason he had sent them to me in a large manila envelope rather than the more conventional method of "email attachment". They were typed up on standard white paper and stuffed into an envelope, about 30 pages in all. On the first page was a yellow post-it note that said:

"Hey Dean,
If you get bored in Africa, here's some reading material.
Dad"

Normally I would have procrastinated a bit longer, maybe read them on the plane ride back home, but I had grown up hearing a lot about the crazy antics of my grandfather and life in the "olden days", so it did have my interest. Also, I had what I could only guess was a full afternoon to kill before we arrived in Dila. So, with no excuses and no other options, I began to read. The first page on the stack was titled "Watermelons, New and Used".

CHAPTER 6
WATERMELONS, NEW AND USED

Late one fall, shortly after Mom and Dad had only been married a very short time, an event occurred which would change the lives of Mom, Dad and all of us kids, forever.

At that time Mom and Dad were starting out, newly married, and were traveling as custom combiners. They would travel the wheat fields through the Midwest with their combine and hire out to local farmers to help bring in the crop. In the early summer the work was in Oklahoma, then Kansas, then Nebraska, and so on progressively north into the Dakotas as the crops began to ripen.

The work was hard. Custom combining meant working from sunup to sundown to bring in the crop. If the crop was ready the farmers wanted it cut and to the elevator before rain or hail or freeze-up which would cause damage. The custom combiner usually had to have a partner; someone to bring him food he could eat while riding the combine, someone to run for fuel and parts, and someone to do the bookwork, pay the bills, and provide a place to sleep and relax. And usually the partner was a wife, and so Mom became part of the custom combine business.

Dad had just finished combining in the fall of 1946 and he and Mom were heading south back to Kansas for the winter. They were pulling a small camper with an old pickup truck as they pulled into a small town in southern

South Dakota for a bit of rest and some gas. There, Dad noticed that a nearby farmer had set up a small melon stand; he also noticed that this farmer had just one of many melon stands scattered up and down the highway.

The melon stand interested Dad; in Kansas melons were so plentiful that there was little profit margin in trying to sell them.

"How much for a melon?" Dad asked.

Dad knew that in Selfridge melons could be had for nearly 75 cents to a dollar, so he was interested in what the difference a couple hundred of miles in distance would make.

"Melons are 15 cents apiece for the small ones and 20 cents for the big ones," the farmer said.

Dad was astonished, 15 cents and 20 cents? In North Dakota these same melons are 75 cents and a dollar! And at that point Dad made a quantum leap; he decided to purchase each and every melon that farmer had for sale.

Mom's only response was, "Homer, Are you crazy?"

But Dad convinced her that money could be made in this venture. After all, wouldn't she like to go back to Selfridge for just a few more days, and more importantly wouldn't she be interested in doubling or tripling their money?

Dad and Mom loaded that little camper and the nearly broken down pickup truck up with every watermelon they could fit into it. Melons were stacked in every room; in the bedroom, on the bed, and in the little living room under the kitchen table and over the sink. When they pulled away from that little South Dakota town they had spent all their summer savings and were headed back north with nearly flat tires on both vehicles.

Dad and Mom went as far as Selfridge and set up shop on an empty corner lot in the downtown business area. Immediately they had success, overwhelming success. All the melons they had, melons purchased only several hundred miles away for only a small price, were sold at a price near four times the cost.

Dad and Mom realized they had discovered a bonanza. If a camper load of melons could so easily be sold in the little town of Selfridge, North Dakota, what was the potential in a bigger town or city, say Mandan or Bismarck to the north.

And in that belief Dad decided to establish himself. On the outskirts of Mandan, ND, Dad purchased land. And on that land Dad built. He built a large (at least we kids remember as large) barn facing the road with an overhang for shade along one entire side. Under that overhang he positioned tables and counters. And in the barn itself he had space to receive, store, sort and manage his product. And his product was fruits and vegetables. Dad had established his business as Royse's Watermelon Kingdom.

In the spring, Dad would bring in melons from as far away as Mexico, then Texas, then Oklahoma, and progressively further north as those crops became ready. While that steady stream of melons continued all summer, Dad also brought in cherries, peaches, and pears from Montana, Idaho, and Oregon; apples and onions from Washington; cantaloupe from Colorado; pumpkins and squash from South Dakota; tomatoes from Arkansas; and numerous other fruits and vegetables from numerous other places in the country.

During that first year Dad and Mom developed a business plan and pattern. There was no analysis by any business advisor, or consultation with any banker, or review by any Board of Directors. The Plan was simple. In those early years Dad would head out with his big semi tractor-trailer, generally with only enough money to put gas in the truck and nothing in his pocket. When Dad was in melon country (or apple country, or whatever he was after) he would make inquiries with local growers or brokers for the produce. The deal Dad offered was simple. Did they have a load of produce they would allow him to take on consignment? Could he take that load to North

Dakota? Of course, there were risks that both parties had to know about. If the produce wasn't good it would be hard to sell; if it was hard to sell then that grower had to know that his return on the produce would be adjusted. And likewise, Dad and Mom would risk possibly donating their time and effort trying to sell produce with no reward for their efforts if it couldn't be sold.

The plan was simple and it worked. Dad would spend the next 40 years or so of his life bringing the produce in and Mom, with help from us kids and occasional hired help, would sell the produce.

Dad was a natural born salesman and that's what it would take to make this plan work. How many growers or farmers would consent to allowing a truck driver from North Dakota, with a barely running and nearly broken down truck, cart off an entire semi-load of produce with nothing more than a promise to pay if the load could be sold. Yet in those first years Dad was successfully able to bring in load after load after load of produce of all types from all locations. And Mom was successful in marketing and selling that produce from a little wooden barn built over swampland, which we all knew as "The Watermelon Kingdom".

Dad was a unique business creature in North Dakota in those days. Who would try to operate an open-air market in a State where produce is generally unavailable except as freighted in and where the weather was so adverse that a load of melons could be lost to frost in May of the year?

Who would think of leaving a wife and small children at home to go out in an old truck, with nearly no money, to try to buy produce from tight fisted growers and farmers on no money down and only a promise to pay?

Dad and Mom made their business a success by pure sweat and determination. In those days of the early to mid-50's there were no federal restrictions of number of hours any one man could operate a truck without rest; consequently Dad became a near full time and around the clock driver. As soon as he brought one load of produce in and was able to unload it, he was back on the road on his way for another load. If he felt tired, he pulled over and slept for a couple hours and if he was hungry he stopped for a hamburger. A time clock and a calendar meant nothing to Dad. And to some extent Mom maintained the same schedule. Every day during the season Mom opened the market at sunup and every day that market stayed open until well past dark. As kids we learned to eat our lunches and dinners between customers and we learned, from example, what the rewards were for hard work and perseverance.

Over the years Dad and Mom became expert produce salesmen and experts in dealing with customers and people. They passed that knowledge on to all us kids to a lesser extent. All of us, at an early age, were expected to work in the stand. We all had to unload those produce trucks as they came in, pick out the ripe and spoiled fruit, set out displays, and wait on customers.

When a load of melons would come in we would form a line of bodies to toss those melons from the truck into the stand. Friends of ours would be recruited to come out from town and be in that unloading line. A typical melon truck might have 2 to 3 thousand melons, each of which had to be individually picked up and tossed from person to person until it got to the "stacker" in the stand. The stacker was the last person in the line and his job was to stack the melons in a neat and orderly arrangement for customer display. Stacking melons is almost an art. Melons come in a variety of shapes and sizes and often vary greatly in those sizes and shapes even within the same load. Some melons, like the Georgia Greys (which actually come from Texas), are longer and narrower and are easily stacked into a pyramid type arrangement. Other melons, such as the Black Diamonds (which actually do come from Texas) are almost perfectly round and seem to defy being placed on top of each other. A good stacker can arrange the melons, in rows, up to eight or nine levels high and in such a manner that as customers remove melons from the stack for purchase, the remainder of the stack does not come tumbling down.

Dad was an expert stacker. He could put odd size and odd shaped and round and oblong melons together in a stack that would look picture perfect.

There were other tricks to the trade that we kids learned from being involved in the family fruit business. Onions had to be covered if it rained, pumpkins would freeze fast at anything below 32 degrees but apples kept best at near 20 degrees, cherries had to be sorted on an almost daily basis, tomatoes are bought green and left to ripen on the shelf, and so on and so on.

When my oldest brother Alex and I were old enough to manage the till, wait on customers and keep the displays up, Dad and Mom devised a work schedule to allow us some free time mixed with our work time at the stand. The day was divided into four separate three-hour shifts; shift-one was generally 9AM to noon; shift-two was noon to 3PM; shift-three was from 3PM to 6PM; and shift-four, the last shift, was from 6PM to closing which was generally at 9PM. Alex and I were expected to work two shifts each; how we arranged or arrived at the shifts on each day was left up to the two of us. If one of us wanted to go to a movie, then the evening shift had to be covered by the other; likewise if one of us wanted to sleep in the next day, then the other had better be at work for the morning shift.

It was a simple process, but in the tradition of our Dad, Alex and I made it as complicated as possible. We never had a set pattern of shifts; often the shifts got divided as the day wore on with neither of us knowing who would be working on any given shift until the time came. On some days one of us (usually me as I recall) might work three or all the shifts, with the other "owing" for some unnamed replacement work. By that method we could work continuous shifts, two or three days at a time, and then have continuous time off, that same two or three days at a time.

Confusing the arrangement even more was the fact that we were being paid by Dad for our shift work. The pay was 50 cents an hour, with an expectation that in any single day each of us would work six hours and earn three dollars. When we started trading shifts and accumulating shifts the pay process got more complicated. On some days Alex would offer to pay me his wage to work his shift if he didn't have to repay the shift to me at a later time. And vice versa, I would make that offer to Alex from time to time.

To this day, according to my records, Alex still owes me three shifts of work, and no, I will not accept payment in full of $1.50 as compensation.

Later after Alex and I went away to college and were able to free ourselves from Dad's shift work, our younger siblings all became involved in the same duties at the store. All of us, by this work, became exposed to dealing with people, visiting with customers, listening to their complaints, and mostly watching Dad and Mom handle those day to day problems. We never saw a problem come up where either had to raise their voices (except to us kids occasionally) or lose their tempers.

On one occasion a pesky (although longstanding) customer couldn't understand why the store didn't offer the melons in halves or quarters. Why did Homer only sell whole melons? It didn't make sense to him; if the stores in town could do it then the Watermelon Kingdom should also be able to?

After this customer had asked and asked and asked and pestered poor Dad to death we expected Dad to just tell him to take his business into town if he had to have a half melon, but Dad was forever calm.

"Sorry," Dad said. "We don't sell melons in half because they're just too hard to haul that way."

And another time we witnessed Mom berate a

customer she had just discovered trying to steal a melon while our backs were turned. The customer in question was a rough looking character that, we were told, had served some time in the State Penitentiary for armed robbery. That detail didn't stop Mom from demanding payment for the melon.

That customer was indignant, "I certainly did not steal that melon. I intended to come back and pay you for it."

But Mom to her credit held her ground and insisted that he was stealing. She told him, just pay for the melon and don't come back.

The ex-convict customer was willing to pay, but just to set the record straight; he insisted Mom give him a paid in full receipt for the melon. Mom was willing to set the record straight too, and the receipt she gave him said "Paid in Full for One Stolen Melon".

Because of the nature of the produce business we always had to deal with interesting customers. Otherwise perfectly normal and pleasant people would stop at the stand and, because it was a roadside stand, believed that the price placed on the merchandise was somehow negotiable. To some extent the prices were negotiable; if a farmer wanted six crates of peaches rather than just a dozen by the bag, Dad was always open to negotiating a special price to that person. By watching both Mom and Dad, day in and day out, deal with people and negotiate sales, and do all those things needed to keep a business alive, all of us kids benefited. Dad was able to tell in the first few seconds if an irritating customer was worth humoring or if it was better just to ignore the fellow.

In addition to dealing with customers all day long, there was also a fairly steady stream of farmers who came out to the stand wanting to sell us their produce. Dad liked to deal with the farmers; they generally had good produce, they never wanted anything but a fair price, and they were willing to trade with him and otherwise do business with him in return. Most often Dad would buy pumpkins, squash and corn from the local people and occasionally someone would come in with a load of river bottom melons. Even if we had a whole store full of a certain item, Dad liked to keep an ongoing trade going with local farmers. It was good business to buy their produce and he knew it.

But just as Dad liked to buy locally, he was very leery of buying produce from truckers who would happen to show up at the store from time to time. Those truckers might have almost anything to sell; it may be a load of melons, or onions, or cantaloupes, or apples, or almost anything else.

Dad sometimes bought those loads but if he did he was cautious. It wasn't uncommon for a load of melons to be sweetened with a few good ones for sampling while the rest of the load was not good. It also wasn't uncommon for produce off the street to be packaged in boxes labeled number-one quality while in fact the actual produce was not to that quality. Dad and Mom both became pretty discerning buyers; samples from a load of melons had to be checked throughout the entire load, phone calls had to be made to the point of origin of each load to verify ownership, and all produce had to be tasted and cut and tasted and cut as it was being unloaded.

Occasionally, despite Dad's best efforts to be careful in purchasing produce we would end up with a bad load. Many times a load of melons or cantaloupes was delivered to the yard, far too ripe with melon juice just running from the trailer. At those times we kids knew we were in for pure torture. Each melon would have to be hand sorted out of that load and wiped dry while the spoiled ones would be set aside for disposal. Those spoiled melons would be oozing, stinking and running all over the entire trailer and all over us, but there was no choice except to do the sorting.

In one instance Dad became the owner of a load of onions, which, after he had purchased them, he realized they were not quite the quality he had hoped for. Rather than trying to sell those onions at the stand Dad had a better idea. He took that trailer load of onions down the road several hundred miles until he came upon the outskirts of a small town. At that point Dad pulled his truck to the side of the road, took a few removable panels out of the trailer (just enough to spill a few bags of onions up and down the road) and then hitchhiked into town. In town Dad had the local paper run an ad.

"Truck Accident West of Town, Trucker Must Sell Load of Onions at Sacrifice Price."

And sell onions Dad did; the entire town came out to get a good deal at supposedly Dad's expense.

No doubt, both Dad and Mom were masters of not only buying and selling produce, but in dealing with human nature.

CHAPTER 7
INJERA WRAPPED INJERA

With a sudden halt, the van abruptly pulled off to the side of the road. The entire car perked up and conversation in Amharic began to fill the air. We of course had no idea what was happening. In our obviously confused state, one of the women turned around to clue us in.

"Lunch," she said, as if it was one of only a few English words she knew.

"Oh great, thank you!" I said, as Ethan took out his headphones to rejoin the world.

"They're stopping for lunch".

"Great! I'm starving. What do they eat here for lunch anyway? Monkey brains?" he said as if he had significantly adjusted his expectations.

"No! Don't be ridiculous. That's more of a breakfast thing," I said sarcastically. "My guess is that lunch today will involve injera in some fashion. But I encourage you to try and order a Spanish omelet or a breakfast burrito and see how well that goes."

"Well, they must have eggs at least right?"

"Eh, don't be so sure."

As we stepped outside the van, we left our big backpacks tied to the roof and kept our smaller bags with us. The restaurant had an outside patio area as well as seating inside. Most people sat at their own tables and scattered evenly around the restaurant but they all ordered the same thing, which probably meant there was only one thing to order.

"So what do you think they serve here?" Ethan asked.

Playing stupid, I just replied, "I don't know, you should check out the menu."

"Oh, hell yeah!" he said with excitement. "They've got pizza! Oh and look, they do have omelets! Told you!" he exclaimed defiantly. "And here you are, trying to pretend it's all about hard living out here! What are you gonna get?"

"I'll probably just have the injera."

"What! Aren't you sick of that stuff by now?

"Yes."

As soon as I replied the waitress came up to take our order. She didn't say anything. She just looked at us.

Ethan immediately but cautiously began to place his order, "Can I have the pizza?"

"No," she shook her head stoically.

Confused, Ethan replied, "Oh, can I have the BLT then?"

"No," she shook her head again.

"Omelet?"

"No."

This could have gone on all day.

"Two injera fir firs please," I interjected.

"Okay," she said smiling, and walked away.

Injera was the Ethiopian staple calorie containing food. It's like bread to the French, rice to the Chinese and tortillas to the Mexicans. It goes with every meal and is made from a fermented corn mash that is pounded into a flat pancake-like shape. From there it's usually eaten with the hands as a way to scoop up whatever else you're eating with it, and usually what you end up eating it with is goat meat.

Ethan had a look on his face that somehow mixed confusion and disappointment.

"Well, what the hell man! Why wouldn't she serve me a

pizza?"

"Because they don't have it. They rarely have all of the stuff on the menu. We're in the country now. It's expensive to ship in smoked salmon or tomatoes or anything that doesn't grow right here."

"Well, what's the point of a menu then? Why do they even have one?" he exclaimed.

"I don't know, maybe they occasionally have those items, maybe it's just good marketing," I said smiling.

This part of Ethiopia was made up almost entirely of subsistence farmers, which meant there wasn't a whole lot of extra money that could be used to purchase exotic outside foods. So the people here, and those traveling through, were usually stuck with whatever was produced locally and a lot of times that was just injera and goat. Based on my experience you can always count on one thing being available whether its stated or not, and that one thing is injera.

"Well, Goddamn it!" Ethan said.

I found his frustration slightly funny.

"So what the hell is injera fir fir anyway? I've never heard of it and I used to live near an Ethiopian restaurant," he said.

"Well, it may not always be served at Ethiopian restaurants in the States. I guess because it's not a dish that you'd really seek out. Think of it as a working man's meal."

"Oh that sounds promising......and?"

"Basically its day-old injera that's covered in a sauce and then wrapped in fresh injera," I said cautiously.

"Are you fucking kidding me?!"

"No, that's injera fir fir. Just try to keep an open mind. It's an adventure, right?"

As our injera fir fir came out, Ethan watched it cautiously as it was placed at our table. The gray injera was in the form of a blob-like mass on the center of the plate and clearly contained something. He poked at it slightly and eventually opened a whole in the side where pieces of the sauce-covered-injera could pour out. He tried a couple bites with a fork and eventually agreed that it wasn't as bad as it sounded...just a little boring. He ended up finishing the whole plate.

During our break we kept a close eye on the van as to not miss its departure, and after about 20 minutes our team was ready to re-board and hit the road. When the rest of the passengers began to assemble around the van we followed suit, and as we boarded the van we each reclaimed our original seat inside.

The ride continued more or less the same as we made our way deeper into the Great Rift Valley. It was dry, dusty and hot and by now we were covered in a sweat and dirt combination that only added to an increasingly uncomfortable situation. The temperature rose gradually as we moved south but the breeze from the moving van kept us from complete misery.

Aside from the gradual flattening of the landscape, our surroundings appeared to change very little throughout the day. As we drove south, Ethan spent most of his time listening to music and staring out the window. But with the roaster still on his lap, he didn't have much room to move. As for me, I found myself slightly hooked on my father's stories. It was interesting to read about how life was back in those days, to see how things have changed and to finally get an understanding of where our family had come from. With a long journey still in front of us I was ready for part two, the second story in the packet. This one was called "Mayor Of The Strip".

CHAPTER 8
MAYOR OF THE STRIP

In the late 1940's when Dad was beginning his produce and trucking business, he decided the place for him and his family would be in the little dusty cowboy town of Mandan, North Dakota. North Dakota was just fine with Dad, after all Mom was from Selfridge, North Dakota, just 70 some miles south, and there were relatives and friends on her side of the family to make him feel welcomed. Besides Dad always said Kansas was just too cold in the winter.

Mandan appealed to Dad. Here was a friendly little town (at that time around 6,000 people) with opportunity. The flavor of the town was blue collar and western; even today the Main Street boasts the Silver Dollar Bar, the Chuck Wagon Cafe, and the Mandan Pioneer news. And for culture and a bit more civilization, the capital of North Dakota, Bismarck, was located just across the river. Being close to a State Capitol appealed to Dad's lifelong interest in politics.

And especially appealing to Dad was "The Strip". At that time, even as today, the stretch of highway between Bismarck and Mandan, was referred to as "The Strip". The Strip is on the Mandan side of the Missouri River and stretches for about 3 miles connecting the east end of Mandan to the Memorial Bridge over the Missouri River. Across that bridge was the city of Bismarck. At that time anyone wanting to go from Bismarck to Mandan, or vice

61

versa, had to travel that strip; likewise anyone traveling cross-country through North Dakota or across the upper Midwest had to be on that highway. The next nearest bridge that allowed you to cross the Missouri River was over 100 miles to the south of the Strip or some near 200 miles to the northwest.

At the time Dad settled on the strip it was only a narrow two lane paved highway. Up and down that highway were various implement dealers, car lots, nightclubs, bars and repair shops. Dad was one of very few to actually maintain a residence in the area. Later in the 1950's a large livestock auction established a sales arena near Dad and later farm supply stores, feed stores, mobile home and recreational dealers, a bowling alley, and an out door theater established themselves in this area.

The strip became known as a central gathering place for farmers and ranchers when they came into the Mandan-Bismarck area. During the day they could bring their livestock to the sale, visit implement dealers, buy hardware and lumber, and conduct all other manners of business on the Strip. At night the business could continue at one of several bars, cafes, or nightclubs, or they could take the family bowling or to an outdoor movie or, if it were summertime, spend an evening at the carnival which always located in one of the many wide open lots along the highway.

On that strip between the two small cities of Mandan and Bismarck Dad figured he had found himself a home. This was away from the city limits of both Mandan and Bismarck yet just between them to afford accessibility for his business venture. It looked to be ideal. Dad purchased a two-three acre plot of land that no one else at that time believed had any value. The land was low and swampy and generally covered with thick brush and scrub trees. To anyone else it looked like a headache; to Dad it looked like an opportunity.

The opportunity that Dad wanted to pursue was a fruit

and vegetable business. Dad and Mom had experienced success in bringing melons up into the Selfridge area just a year or two prior and Dad was convinced that the Strip between two towns would also be successful. Besides, Dad was from Kansas where it was common to drive down the road and see roadside produce stands and markets, often every quarter or half mile, one after the other. If those stands, one after the other after the other, could make money for their owners then it would seem that a fruit stand in North Dakota, of which there were none anywhere, should be successful.

And to compliment the fruit business Dad also believed that this venture on the Strip should be a complete farm to market business. Dad would continue to run his own trucks and trailers and haul all his own produce to the Strip.

In later years Dad's instincts of the desirability of the land was proven. The Government built a Dam on the River and flooding was nearly eliminated as a concern. After the Dam was built, more and more businesses decided to locate on the Strip. Later the City of Mandan annexed the Strip (now it was officially "Memorial Highway") and the old two-lane State highway was widened into a five-lane expressway. The City installed water and sewer services to the residences and business's (in fact it wasn't until 1974 that Dad and Mom finally got indoor plumbing) and other City amenities soon followed. There were new streetlights installed, the highway began to be regularly plowed in the winter, and soon after, a new golf course and racecar arena were constructed along the highway.

Through all of this change there remained The Watermelon Kingdom. By this time the original green wood barn structure had been removed and replaced with a wood structure with roll up garage doors facing the highway. An overhang, nearly doubling the size of the building, was added to the east side of the building, and later large loading docks for the trucks were added both on the east and west ends of the structure. Off the back, used primarily for truck storage and repair was a large metal building which also had a loading dock and also attached to the main wooden produce building.

The nature of Dad's business, from conception, involved both produce and trucking. To be successful in produce, Dad believed you had to haul it yourself and be absolutely assured of freshness. Dad believed that customers liked the idea of fresh produce, right off the truck, that they could watch being unloaded as they bought it. And to be successful in the trucking business Dad believed you often had to forgo new and expensive equipment and often rely on older and used equipment.

And rely on older equipment he did. It almost became his trademark that he would rather run an old truck and trailer down the road than "put up" with any newer equipment. A part of the strategy of using older equipment was keeping a large inventory of old truck parts and pieces on hand. If a truck broke down, which happened all the time, Dad was almost always able to go back into his truck bone-pile and find the piece needed to put that truck back on the road.

Dad was the master of keeping old parts on hand. If any piece of equipment finally hit that point of no repair (often that point was a fine line which only Dad could determine) then Dad would usually drag it around behind and make it a "parts vehicle". His collection of parts grew; in that back yard, which grew over the years from two acres to nearly eight acres, Dad slowly built an inventory of rows and rows of disabled trucks, trailers, vans, and all combinations thereof. At times he even had school buses, earthmoving equipment, boom trucks, and other such items in his collection. If any of his functioning trucks needed a part, almost any part, Dad could usually find it in his private inventory. And that kept the trucks running, and kept the produce coming, and that drew the customers. And that was Dad's business, working just as he had planned it.

Unfortunately, while it was true that the Dad's business plan was on track, Dad came into a conflict with the plan and the vision of the City of Mandan for the Strip. Mandan, although having a history of being a blue collar, working man's town, was slowly trying to change its image. Mandan was striving to be like Bismarck across the river; white collar, refined, and respectable. After all, the City had annexed the Strip, had renamed it to Memorial Highway, had widened the road, provided water and sewer, and had built a municipal golf course in the area. The City could understand sand and water traps on that golf course but couldn't reconcile themselves to scrap metal and truck part traps, all of which was on Dad's land just adjacent to their new course.

Mandan formed a community betterment committee, the role of such committee to be to identify areas within the City of Mandan that should be cleaned up. And that committee took particular interest in the back yard of Homer Royse.

Dad was notified, in writing one day, that the City would like him to clean up his yard in 30 days. Dad responded the way we all knew he would; he threw the notice away. To him it was a joke. Why would he want to eliminate his truck parts inventory? And even if he did, who believed that 30 plus years of accumulation could be moved in 30 days?

A few months went by and the City again notified Dad, again in writing, now they required him to clean his yard. After all, they told him, they had "pictures"; they could verify that there were areas that contained vehicles in a "non-working or disabled condition". And of course Dad laughed again just as we knew he would. Pictures? Was that some sort of threat or was this a joke?

As Dad put it, "Maybe I'll ask them to send me copies, I'd like to use some for Christmas cards this year."

Dad again responded by throwing the notice away.

The notifications may have been amusing for Dad but they were nerve-racking for the rest of the family. We all figured, well maybe we should clean up, avoid bad publicity, create a better business atmosphere, etc., etc.

Mom put it best, "Homer! Are you crazy? Why do you want to fight with the City?"

Dad insisted he wasn't about to jump just because somebody in the City said so. He had been there for years (nearly 30 by this time) and "the county never bothered me with this" and "the customers don't care what's out back" and "the truck parts are already away from the highway and out of sight" so what was the big deal? No, he wasn't going to move anything; he was right in this issue and if the City wanted to argue and fight then he would argue and fight.

After some time went by and Dad had still not responded to any of the City's notices (other than tearing them up and throwing them away) another written notice arrived in the mail. We knew this was an important notice because it arrived certified mail. The City was requesting Dad to appear before the next City Commission Meeting for a "visit" regarding his back yard.

Mom was frantic. Ruin was imminent. She could envision the City making a sweeping proclamation "Today is Designated as Clean Homer's Yard Day", and she believed the TV news cameras would be leading with Dad's yard story. Something along the line as "Hurricane Agnes Destroys Florida; North Dakota Secedes From the Union; and Homer Royse Fights City Hall...News at 11."

Of course Dad was calm. He really couldn't care less. If the City wanted him to come in for a visit, well sure, Dad would go in for a visit. Visiting was part of selling, and selling was what Dad did best.

On the day Dad was to make his appearance before the City it was a typical busy day at the market. In the morning the trucks and drivers had to be gotten out, produce was being delivered and had to be unloaded, and the phone rang all day long with a thousand details for Dad to attend to. By late afternoon Dad was running late in his daily schedule and he had missed his noon lunch. So Dad, on his way into town to meet with the City, still running behind on time but not overly concerned, stopped at the local Dairy Queen for quick ice cream cone. An ice cream cone, quick and easy, seemed like a good idea to tide him over until supper.

When Dad got to the City Hall he still had that cone; he had only been able to eat a little bit of it since the Dairy Queen. And as everyone knows, you can't leave a nearly complete ice cream cone in a car, especially on a hot day and especially when it may be some time before you would be back. Dad did what he believed was logical; he took the cone, now dripping slightly, into the meeting with him.

"Well," the mayor begins, looking at Dad and his dripping ice cream cone. "Nice to see you, etc. etc.…thanks for coming in, etc. etc.…and what steps are you willing to take to help us get your yard cleaned up?"

Dad goes to the front of the room to the speaker's podium. All eyes are on him and especially on his dripping ice cream cone. The City Commissioners are confused. This is a formal City meeting; who would bring an ice cream cone to a formal meeting? And didn't Homer Royse realize that the cone was dripping on their new carpet just put in only a month or so before? Maybe this was a negotiating tactic; they had heard Homer Royse was a shrewd negotiator.

Dad was calm. He didn't mind talking to the City Commissioners and he didn't mind his cone dripping on their new carpet. Dad stated he didn't believe his yard was any different now than it had been in the last 20 or so years but, if it would help, he would agree to move some things around and rearrange. The cone continues to drip on that new carpet.

"But you've got rows and rows of tires and wheels out

there that you're not using and they don't look good for anything," and, the Commissioners added, "We've got pictures."

"No," Dad says. "Those tires and wheels I need. If I have a flat tire on an old truck I may not want to buy a new tire. A new tire might cost more than the truck is worth. So I need my old tires and wheels and everything else that's out there."

"What about the truck cabs and trailer bodies and other vehicles that aren't running? They can't be good for much!"

"Those I need too. The trailers I use for storage and the truck cabs I use for parts. Besides, on a lot of those cabs and trailers there's money owed to the bank so I can't move them even if I wanted to."

At this point Dad is still calm, leaning against the podium with a steady stream of melted ice cream running down to the floor. The discussion is now on its last legs; the Commissioners see that Dad is not going to move too much stuff if any at all. They also see that Dad is willing to stand there the rest of the afternoon and calmly discuss the issue. Their worst fear is that if they take a recess to discuss this, Dad may go out and buy another cone.

An agreement of sorts appears to be reached. The City is concerned with unsightly areas, especially as can be viewed from the new golf course area. Dad believes that the parts and pieces he has collected are needed for his business. It is agreed that Dad will do some remedial cleaning but Dad will retain those parts he feels he needs.

And on that general understanding the visit was concluded.

When Dad got home Mom wanted to know exactly what happened.

"Not too much," Dad said. "I told them I needed the stuff and it wasn't junk and they said 'okay'. Besides they were really more interested in a little ice cream on their carpet then they were me."

After about a year had gone by, and Dad had still not removed any of his parts and pieces, the phone rang one day.

"Mr. Royse," a secretary said. "The Mayor of the City himself wants to visit your yard and see what you've accomplished."

At that time the mayor "himself" was a local fellow who also happened to drive a milk truck.

Dad replied, "I'm the Mayor out here and there's no need for a visit unless I need a quart of milk. I'll let you know."

End of conversation.

The letters from the City continued after that exchange. Dad continued to throw the letters away and to leave his yard the way he wanted it. He just firmly believed that if he was paying taxes on the land, which he was, and if he needed the truck parts and pieces to run his business, which he believed he did, then he just wasn't going to be pushed around by the City in this matter. A point in time came when Dad had to hire a local attorney to represent him with the City in the issue; apparently after the ice cream cone visit they weren't interested in any more negotiations with Dad.

The City had been, apparently for some time, enforcing some cleanup provision against other businesses on the Strip with threats of legal action. The City probably reasoned; who would spend money on an attorney to protect what they believed was a junk pile?

Dad's hiring of an attorney to deal with the City had the desired effect. Now if the City wanted to take "pictures" they had better have permission. Now if statements were made regarding "junk" they had better be prepared to prove it as junk. And now if Dad would suffer any business damage because of the issue, the City had better be prepared to compensate Dad for that damage. The City quietly and immediately stopped sending letters and requests to Dad for yard cleanup.

Interestingly, Dad's fight with the City began shortly after Mandan had annexed the Strip around 1972.

The letters and requests and visits between Dad and the City carried on intermediately through the 70's and into the mid-80's, up until Dad retained his attorney.

Every time a new mayor took office in Mandan, a letter could be counted on to soon follow. And with each new mayor in Mandan, Dad had to remind those City fathers that they may run the City, but he was still the mayor of the strip.

CHAPTER 9
DILA

As the sun began to set, we found ourselves in the first overnight stop on our journey. We had arrived at our destination for the day, the transit hub of Dila.

The van dropped us all off on the main street and then pulled away around the corner, probably to rest for the night and then head back north to Addis the next day. Everyone, aside from the two of us, knew exactly where they were headed and proceeded in doing so. We however, took a minute to stand there slightly dumbfounded as if we were waiting for someone to make our next move for us. It was dark, quiet and we were surely out of our element on the side of that dirt road.

Within seconds one of our fellow passengers walked back toward our direction. He was an older man who wore a red suit coat and a dusty black pinstriped fedora. He had a short grey beard and carried an old fashioned piece of luggage like something out of the 1970's or 80's. For some reason his appearance made me think of him as a New Orleans trumpet player, although I'm certain in reality he did something very different. Probably noticing that we were lost, alone and looking perplexed, he decided to help us out.

"Hotel," he said as he pointed to a long house on a back road.

"Oh thank you!" I said. "Let's follow this guy."

We followed our newly adopted guide to what, based

on the size of the town, had to be the only hotel in operation. It was only a few meters from where we were dropped off, but set back slightly behind the main road. The building itself was a long thin complex made up of hotel rooms all in a row with the doors to the rooms opening directly to the outside. There was no front desk or reception area, just a man sitting on a wooden stool outside one of the rooms wearing a pair of old brown dress pants and a dirty "wife-beater" undershirt. He appeared to be focused mostly on chewing his bushel of chat rather than renting any rooms, but he perked up as we approached him.

Our new guide made first contact with the man on the wooden stool and seemed to settle on a price fairly quickly as if it wasn't their first time meeting. There was a tone of understood compliance and our newly adopted guide waved us goodbye as he made his way to his room a few doors down.

We followed suit in an attempt to negotiate a fair price, but the man's first price was 100 Birr, the equivalent of $5 USD, for a room with two twin beds and a nightstand. It was hard to argue with that, especially when he was probably the only shop in town. So we took it, no questions asked. Our room was number three, two doors down from the man on the wooden stool.

The hotel amenities came complete with an outside "toilet" which was basically an outhouse with a hole in the ground, a "bucket-bath" and a single condom placed on the nightstand. The "single condom on the night stand" was a surprisingly common feature of budget hotels in Ethiopia.

The "bucket-bath" consisted of a giant black plastic tub that looked like it was set up to collect rainwater. It was sitting next to another outhouse with a cement floor. Inside the outhouse was a large bucket with a small cup inside it. A classic "bucket-bath" set up.

A "bucket-bath" is accomplished by filling up one large

bucket with water, usually rain or well water, and then using the smaller cup to poor water over your body. It's really not too bad and tends to save a lot of water but us westerners sometimes have trouble adapting.

Ethan was significantly less impressed with our hotel than I was. He simply smoked a cigarette on the porch steps leading up to the entrance of our room while listening to his music. I was starting to get the feeling Ethiopia was not agreeing with him but we said nothing about it.

Eventually we settled in, locked our hotel room door and ventured out to find dinner. Back at the main intersection where we were originally dropped off, we found a small restaurant and a corner store that sold sodas, biscuits and sambusas.

A "sambusa" is the African version of the Indian "Samosa", which is a deep fried triangular pastry filled with spiced vegetables or meat, a slightly different name but equally as good.

"So, what do you think? Restaurant or corner store?" I said as we stood in the road staring at our options.

"Well, the restaurant looks like it's closing, so I say corner store. It's also faster and I need to sleep."

Ethan's second day in Ethiopia ended as it began, with the two of us sitting on a street corner, this time eating four pieces of sambusa and drinking two cans of orange Fanta. As we ate, we stared out onto the street in front of us. It was quiet, dark and peaceful. The only signs of life were from a few dimly lit rooms that were scattered along the main road where people piled in together to watch low budget sitcoms before going to bed. In these small towns, the day usually ends shortly after the sun goes down. In this case, we were not complaining.

After eating our dinner we stumbled back to the hotel room in the darkness. Outside of the main road, the rest of the town was nearly pitch black as if electricity had been cut from all "non-essential" areas. We used a headlamp to find our hotel and see our way into the room. No matter; we were tired and nothing sounded better than lying down and sleeping in a bed. No teeth brushing, no bucket-bath, we were out for the night.

***

The following day had begun with a question, "How do we get out of Dila"? As lovely as it was to sit and sip orange Fanta by the roadside, we had already soaked up all that the town had to offer us.

We just naturally woke up early and had a brief conversation with our hotel manager. We had found out that a bus was scheduled to pass through Dila at around 11am. This of course meant that it would actually probably pass through Dila at around 1PM, but we, as clueless foreigners, had to be ready for the 11AM arrival rather than miss our chance. Luckily this still allowed plenty of time for breakfast and a bucket-bath.

"So what will it be this morning? Will you be having the injera, sambusa or bananas?" I said excitedly, as we stood near the same street corner where we had our dinner the night before…again, contemplating our options.

"Ah hell! I'll just have two sambusas and a coffee. Do they have coffee?"

"Of course! This is Ethiopia. They always have coffee! That, you can be sure of."

Something Ethiopia does very well, and probably better than anywhere else in the world, is coffee. Coffee has been grown here as long as humans have cultivated it, and it has become an integral part of the culture. What makes it so good is not only the beans but the unique way that it's prepared.

To brew a proper Ethiopian cup of coffee, first you take raw coffee beans and hand roast them in a pan before each brew. Once roasted black, they are crushed into a fine powder and put into a large liquid container. Hot water is then added and the residue is allowed to settle. What results is a perfectly prepared cup of tasty, and very strong Ethiopian coffee. The preparation process is referred to as a "Coffee Ceremony".

Unfortunately, that style of coffee was not available in this town. Instead we drank two cups of NesCafe instant coffee. Irony.

As we sat on two red plastic chairs outside the corner store, we enjoyed our sambusas and coffee and looked out onto our first real experience of Dila. I had seen Ethiopia up close in the week's prior, but that was the northern historical route. This region of Ethiopia was far less traveled which meant for us, a more authentic experience of real everyday life.

The street began to slowly come alive, at least as much as a small town can. People would stroll by at a leisurely pace with their eyes usually fixed on the two strangers sitting at the town's main hub. Sometimes we would get a "hello" or maybe just a wave and a smiling face. Either way, the pace of life here was nicer, more relaxed and welcoming. It wasn't every day that two strangers stopped by to have a coffee in Dila.

Across the street near our hotel I could see a small boy playing with a toy in the dirt road. He was alone and pushing a small car with a wooden stick. The small car that he was pushing was actually only a 12oz soda bottle with pins stuck through it for axels and bottle caps for wheels. On the rear of the bottle he had attached the wooden stick with which he used to push it. He was alone, smiling and seemed happy as he made "car noises" to make his car come alive. It made me think about how much we have in the West, how much more we think we need, and how much children, whether rich or poor, don't often give a shit.

"Okay! Wanna shower up and get ready to go?" I said enthusiastically.

"Yes, please! Where are the showers anyway? I didn't

see them."

"Well they don't exactly have showers in the traditional sense, but they do have a bucket-bath."

"And what in God's name is that?" he said with a look of utter disappointment as if he could envision the process unfolding.

After I graciously explained the bucket-bath concept on our walk back to the hotel and assured him that he would surely survive it, we were able to get cleaned up, checked out and waiting by the side of the road by 11:15am. Fifteen minutes late, but still early by African time.

And there we were, both of us sitting on our bags under a tree on the side of the road nearby to where the boy was playing with the homemade car just hours before. By the looks on our faces it would have been obvious that we were far less enthused than the boy had been. But then again adults tend to adopt certain expectations over time, even in foreign places. Luckily for us we had two orange Fantas on reserve and a couple of iPods with full charges.

As we sat staring at the dirt road in front of us we noticed a strange site off in the distance. Was it a mirage? It appeared to be approaching us. As it got closer I could tell that it wasn't just one, but two girls. Two blonde girls! And they were walking our way.

"Hey boys!" said the first girl.

"Hey!" I said, trying to hold back my enthusiasm. "We're doing good…just waiting for our bus to Moyale."

"Moyale?! Wow, I've heard that's a rough road down that way. Why ya headed there?"

"Well, we're slowly working our way to the beach. Diani beach, in Kenya."

"Let's hope it's not too slow!" Ethan interjected.

"Haha! Tired of traveling in Ethiopia? I can't blame you for that; it's not so easy."

"What are you girls doing here?" Ethan asked the tall blond.

"We work in south Sudan, but now we're on a bit of a

holiday so we're on our way to the Bati Market out east."

The shorter blond jumped into the conversation. "I hate to break it to you guys but the bus to Moyale isn't coming today."

"What?" I said, as the immediate threat of an entire day wasted in Dila came barreling into reality. "We were told if we wait here the bus would be coming by!"

"Sure that's true, just not today. It runs every other day, so you'll have to wait until tomorrow."

"Goddamn it!" Ethan shouted. "Now what?" he looked at me.

The tall blond wasted no time. "Listen, we're in the same boat as you. We can't get anywhere close to Bati until tomorrow. So, we're off to try and find some beers if you'd like to join us?"

It looked as if she was specifically addressing Ethan as she said this.

A smile immediately appeared on Ethan's face, as if he was transported into a whole new world. A world filled with cute blonde girls, no competition and cheap beer.

"Well, that sounds like a great plan! If we're stuck here for another day let's make the most of it," he exclaimed.

And like that our plans changed. When backpacking it's important to be flexible when things don't go according to plan, but when a couple of cute blond girls ask you to have drinks with them, it's required.

We spent the rest of the afternoon outside a small market that served up ice-cold St. George beers for dirt-cheap. The owner was able to set up a table, umbrella and a few chairs for us so we could have a "home base" while we wasted away the rest of the day. It was right around the corner from our hotel and right on the main road, a good vantage point just in case a bus did decide to roll through town.

Over the passing hours we learned all about our new friends. They were from Finland and living in south Sudan. They were working on a project sponsored by the United

Nations in a town just east of Juba that tried to help refugees on the periphery of the Darfur conflict by providing food, shelter and schooling.

"The situation is so fucked!" the shorter girl proclaimed. "It just seems like with every step forward, we go two steps back."

"What do you mean?" I replied.

"It feels like for every program we run, hundreds of new people keep showing up every month. We just can't keep up. On top of that, our available funds keep getting smaller each month because people in the West start to forget about the problem."

"Wow," I said.

"On top of that, I'm really starting to question some of the work we're doing, like if that money could be better spent elsewhere. They come for the food and shelter, sure. But the education that we provide is often met with so much resistance. Do you have any idea how much time each week I spend trying to convince parents that they need to educate their children? It's crazy, but I'm starting to wonder…do they? Do they really need to? For what? So they can leave home and get a job in a factory or office? I'm just not sure that's any better."

"That may be, but at the end of the day you're working with refugees who've had their whole lives turned upside down. Regardless of any philosophical questions on education, those people need someone there right now. Education or not, I'd guess that it's helping."

"I guess that's true," she said, trying to force a smile.

Like most volunteers or aid workers in Africa they started out optimistic and full of ambition but over time reality washes that away. It's the same disappointment they all have when they realize their efforts and their ideas about saving Africa go unrealized. Whether it's due to limited resources or misguided funds; this isn't a place where problems can be fixed overnight by a couple of girls on a "voluntourism" trip. But I would never say that to them, after all I'm not stupid. In the end, I didn't have the all answers either and I surely wasn't busy saving the world.

After hours of talking, drinking, eating and comparing Africa stories, the market closed down, Ethan and the tall blond left to "take a walk" at which point the short blond and I went back to our hotel to find a cigarette. We sat out on the steps outside my room and talked for an hour before going inside.

The next morning she was gone and in her place was Ethan laying in the twin bed next to mine. Their bus to Bati was scheduled to leave Dila at 5AM and they were surely on their way there by now. During our encounter we had never even exchanged names, but when I awoke I found stuffed in my guidebook a hotel business card and on the back, written in pencil, was her email address. It was signed "Mariana" with a smiley face.

After dragging ourselves out of bed, we completed our morning ritual of bucket-baths, sambusas and coffee and made our way to the side of the road, this time by 11:30AM.

Two hours had come and gone without so much as a single vehicle passing by, when all of a sudden from out in the distance we could hear the honking of a proper African bus. The big kind that makes you fear for your life when you see one of them speeding toward you. We both jumped to our feet to peer off into the distance and sure enough, barreling down the dusty dirt road was a massive, quickly approaching, smog spewing bus. Just what we were looking for!

As it approached, its appearance became more apparent. Despite being covered in dirt, it was painted in a sparkling blue color and had an adornment of sacred flowers placed on its front grill for good luck. It also had a very out-of-place decal on its front window in bold white lettering that simply said "Lil Wayne". That, to me, was as good a sign as any.

As the bus slowed to a stop, we approached the door, verified that it was in fact going south to Moyale, paid our fare and made our way toward two empty spots in the back. We tried to settle in for what was probably going to be a long journey. Ethan put in this headphones and I pulled out the next story in the manila envelope. I rested my head against the window as I began to read. And just like that, we were south bound once again.

CHAPTER 10
RICK STEALS A WATCH

Homer seemed to like to engage with the borderline of society in his business; these were folks that were not particularly dealt the best hand in the card game of life but made their own way by playing the hand they had. Those were the ones who sometimes had to do a little bluffing, and a little risk taking to gain ground. Much like Homer himself.

Homer also enjoyed interaction with such folks because it seemed, for some odd reason; they enjoyed his brand of humor and mischief. If he could enlist a partner in some form of trickery against the establishment (read: government agencies, regulatory, even law enforcement such as highway patrol, or big business) and gain some small victory against those folks, well that was great fun and great sport.

And if Homer could also practice his mischief on unsuspecting employees and other associates, that also was good sport.

With that background it is easy to see why and how Rick came to work with Homer and why and how Homer enjoyed having Rick around. Rick was a young man who came looking for a job when he was still in his late teens. He was borderline employable, had been in a youth correction institute at one time, did not really have a home or supportive family, no special skills, no money, and not a lot going for him except being likable, willing to work, willing to work cheap, and best of all, a little gullible. And, interestingly, Rick had only one good eye with the other being a glass eye.

Homer liked him immediately and he became Homer's de facto sidekick and right hand man for nearly the next 50 years. There were times when Rick would leave for better opportunity or more money, or a little respect, but those times never lasted and Rick always came back to Homer. Like a moth to a flame.

Homer started Rick on a truck as a driver, one glass eye notwithstanding. Homer from the day the association started, always introduced Rick as "Rick with one i". Homer and "One i Rick" became a well-known truck driving team in the early years of Homer's business; they would make trips as a driving team from ND to all parts of the United States in search of produce to bring back to the family market back in Mandan, North Dakota.

On one such trip the episode occurred which Homer for years afterwards would refer to as "Rick Steals a Watch". As Homer and Rick traveled with the truck, Homer never carried much cash; simply didn't have it. He had to rely on his wife Greta to generate cash from produce sales on any given day and then wire funds to him at various truck stops as he needed money. Being always short on cash meant always being hungry, on the verge of near starvation, or so Rick thought. This episode began in that setting; Homer and Rick short on cash, Rick believing he was starving, and Homer looking to impose mischief on poor Rick.

As they pulled into a truck stop late at night in some small town in the middle of Oklahoma, Homer went into the truck stop office to pick up funds waiting there from Greta. Those funds were sufficient to fill the truck for another day with fuel and allow both Homer and Rick to have a meal. But Homer was feeling mischievous and perhaps a little worn by Rick complaining of hunger for all the day and for most of the trip.

And thus a scheme was hatched.

Homer came out of the office with the cash and the following then transpired:

Homer: "Well, bad news. Greta didn't have a very good day and wasn't able to send much money. Looks like we don't have enough money for food and gas."

Rick: "What? I'm hungry. Homer, I have to eat or I can't drive."

Homer: "Well, let's do this. Give me your watch and I'll pawn it for fuel and some hamburgers and then when we come back this way in few days we can get your watch back."

Rick: "My watch? I need my watch. What if they don't take it? What if we can't get it back in a few days?"

This line of objection went on for some time with Rick objecting to having to pawn his watch, and complaining of his hunger, and with Homer offering soothing and reassuring logic that this was completely reasonable. Trade a watch for fuel and hamburgers. Finally either Homer or hunger wore Rick down and he reluctantly gave the watch to Homer to go and make the trade with the truck stop.

"But," Rick said, "be sure you get a receipt so I can get it back in a few days."

Homer, now leaving toward the truck stop office with Rick's watch, "If I don't come back out in few minutes you can assume they took the watch and you can then start fueling the truck."

At that point, Homer with both Rick's watch, and money from Greta in his pocket, went into the truck stop, paid for a couple hamburgers to go, using the cash not the watch, and then paid for the fuel, now in the truck, again with cash, not with the watch. Homer then left the truck stop office with the hamburgers to go, with the watch in his pocket.

As they ate the hamburgers, Homer started a discussion again with Rick, "You know, I didn't like that guy in the office. He took the watch but he said you looked like a punk kid, not too smart looking, and I should be careful of you."

Rick: "What, he said what?"

"He said you were a punk and not very bright looking. That may be true but I sure didn't like him saying that."

Now Rick is upset: "A punk kid! I ain't no punk kid. Not smart looking! I'm smart looking!"

And now the hook was set.

"Well even if you are a punk and not very smart looking I just don't like this guy saying that about you. I think we're going to get even with him. Here is what I want you to do. You pull the truck around to the front; I'm going to go in there and grab your watch back and we're going to get this fuel and food for nothing."

And by now Homer had a willing accomplice; willing, angry and looking to get one over on the truck stop that has labeled him as a punk and not very smart looking. So Rick did exactly as he was told, as Homer went back inside the truck stop Rick pulled the truck up front, engine running, and ready to go.

Almost immediately Homer came running out from the truck stop, and jumped in the truck, "Go, go, go! I've got the watch and they are coming after us."

Now don't lose the thread to this story; recall the watch was never traded, was always in Homer's pocket, and there was no actual appropriation of fuel and food without payment. But Rick did not know that.

Rick immediately gunned the truck and tore out of the lot; Homer continuing to look back in the mirror and keeping poor Rick on edge.

"Hurry, Hurry, Hurry, it looks like they may be coming after us!"

And Rick continued to "hurry, hurry, hurry", barreling away from the scene of the perceived crime and absolutely not wanting to be caught.

After a few minutes, with Homer continuing to watch the mirrors for pursuit, things started to calm down.

Homer reached in his pocket and says, "Here's your watch, I told you we would get this back for you; that will keep that guy from making comments about the next punk who comes in there."

And Rick is saying, "Wow, I can't believe you did that! Wow, that was great, that will teach that guy!"

Homer, feeling relaxed in his amusement said, "Only thing may be that I gave them your name on the pawn ticket so that could be an issue if they report this to the police."

"What! You gave my name! You gave my name! They're going to find me; they're going to arrest me! You gave my name!"

Poor Rick was clearly agitated as it now is dawning on him that this perhaps is not the clean getaway as he first thought.

For years after this, as Homer told the "Rick With One i, Who Stole the Watch" story, Rick would always be in complete agreement not to stop at this particular truck stop lest they recognize him and arrest him. For those times when Homer and Rick would stop, Homer would always have poor Rick conceal himself in the truck while Homer went inside, had a leisurely visit with other truckers, and ate a warm meal, with a cold one in the bag for Rick.

Poor Rick, with one i. Crime does not pay.

CHAPTER 11
SPEED BUMPS

Like being awoken from a trance, I was suddenly being tossed around inside the bus. I could hardly stay sitting in my seat as a continued series of thumps kept shaking me off the seat and closer to the floor.

"What the hell is that?" Ethan said as he tore off his headphones.

"I don't know! Is he hitting something?"

To investigate, I poked my head out the side of the window. Due to what seemed like a very strange choice in road design, speed bumps had been placed along this specific stretch of highway. But even stranger was that the bus driver didn't seem to be acknowledging them. He simply sped down the road while ramming over a speed bump every two seconds. This repetitive hitting was causing all the passengers to fly off their seats with each impact. The first few hits seemed to put everyone in a bit of pain but after some careful repositioning and anticipation, the passengers on the bus all began to laugh as if it was an amusement park ride. For a while it was an entertaining spectacle to see an entire bus full of people being thrown up off their seats every few seconds.

However, it didn't take long for the passengers' amusement to turn into annoyance. Within minutes a light fixture fell out of the ceiling and shattered on the floor of the bus but still the driver made no attempt to slow down. Some of the people started to look worried, babies started crying and the chatter in the bus began to increase. I'd say Ethan and I were annoyed as well, but "shock and disbelief" would probably be a better way to describe it. The expressions on peoples' faces led me to believe that this was slightly unusual…but only slightly.

At around the 30-minute-mark there was a halting *thud* from the front of the bus followed by a slight incline in the tilt of the vehicle. Sure enough we had blown a tire. This sort of thing might be expected from racing a 20-ton bus over a series of speed bumps but apparently the driver was betting against it. As we slowly pulled over I could see the same expression on all the faces of the passengers, an unspoken communication that everyone had expected this exact scenario. There were a number of people shouting in Amharic in what seemed like an attempt to get an explanation for the mishap, but we couldn't be certain. Although what we were certain of was that we were stranded in southern Ethiopia, in the middle of nowhere, in the hot sun. I had to wonder what the standard protocol for a situation like this might be.

Casually the bus driver pulled over onto the side of the road and stopped the engine. With the engine off and no breeze flowing through the cabin, the temperature inside became nearly unbearable within seconds. Immediately we evacuated the bus and did our best to find a shady spot near the side of the road. With only a few trees close by, the most popular area was just along side the bus in its ten-foot shadow. There we were sitting somewhere between Dila and the Kenyan boarder on the side of the road with only a few farmers off in the distance to witness our misfortune. So everyone did the only natural thing they could do…. go into the bushes and take a much-needed piss.

Once the bathroom break was over and there was nothing left to do, we sat down with the rest of our crew and huddled underneath the shadow of the bus in an attempt to avoid the brutal Ethiopian sun. Looking out onto the countryside it appeared that the vegetation was becoming lusher in comparison to the drier areas up north. It was still hot and still dry but slightly less so. This, for some reason, felt reassuring to me as we sat there just staring into the horizon, unsure if they had any way to repair the flat tire.

"Okay, this is officially ridiculous!" Ethan declared angrily. "What do we do now?"

"I have no idea."

"You have no idea? What do you mean? What do people do in this situation? There's nothing out here!" he said frantically.

"I agree."

"Oh good, you agree!" he said sarcastically. "That helps!"

"Listen, there's no point in freaking out. We'll just do what everyone else does. I'm sure there's a plan in place."

"I'm glad you're so sure! 'Cause I'm pretty sure that we're going to get picked apart by vultures after dying of heat stroke."

It wasn't like Ethan to get so upset. He was usually a pretty calm guy but he was probably suffering from a bit of culture shock. People can sometimes get a little agitated when that happens.

Trying to escape the situation, he wasted no time putting his headphones back in. As for me, I took pleasure in drinking what was left of my orange Fanta and eating a couple of tiny African bananas that I happened to have on hand. For some reason the small bananas were so much better than the big ones we had back home. My theory was that the flavor, due to the smaller size, was condensed and therefore intensified. Maybe I had too much time to think on these long bus rides.

With no usable spare tire available, our crew of what was nearly 30 people were still sitting and starting off into the landscape. Minutes slowly turned to hours with no change in our situation. Then, from out of nowhere, a horse and carriage appeared on the horizon. It was moving far slower than any motor vehicle would, and as a result, traveled close to the shoulder of the road. The man steering sat on top of the carriage sprawled out as if he'd been riding a long time and needed to periodically readjust his position. His rickety wooden carriage was small and pulled by one tired looking horse. As he slowly approached us, he pulled over to speak with our bus driver. His shirt and pants were tattered and ripped but his teeth were bright white and his smile, big and friendly. He was clearly heading south, but to where, we didn't know. Although it didn't much matter, we were 30 stranded people and he was one guy with a horse and carriage.

The bus driver approached the man on the carriage and the two spoke for a few minutes as they looked at the wheel of the bus and then over to our group crouched next to it. We didn't know what was decided but we could tell a conclusion had been reached by the tone of their voices. The driver quickly walked over to us, grabbed my bag from the side of the bus and began to carry it toward the wooden carriage.

"Come," he said, in an urgent tone.

"What? Where are we going?

"You will go with him. He will take you to Moyale. Okay?"

"Ahhh, okay. That's great, but what about everyone else? How are they getting to Moyale?" I asked.

"It's okay. We will wait for the next bus to come. Here, you go!"

"Really? How much do we pay him?" I asked.

"Not necessary. We have agreed that he will help you. You are guests to Ethiopia," he said with a smile as he threw Ethan's bag onto the back of the carriage. I looked over at the carriage driver who was still smiling as if to welcome us aboard his vessel.

We jumped on the back of the carriage reluctantly, not knowing if we should offer our spots to someone else or just sit quietly and comply. We chose to keep our mouths shut and do what we were told rather than risk insulting their hospitality.

As we waved "goodbye" to our fellow travelers it was with a sense of appreciation and guilt. They were sure to be waiting there for hours more, but the smiles on their faces would have never led you to believe it. In my prior travels I had been used to receiving everything for a price...and usually a well inflated price. But here in rural Africa, where people lived in some of the world's harshest conditions, you could find some of the most generous people.

It made me wonder why that generosity didn't seem to exist elsewhere. Was it a survival mechanism? If you don't work together, you don't survive? Or was it just that the rest of us had lost something very "human" about ourselves over our years of so-called development, as we separated ourselves from our neighbors and the natural environment? As we've poured into cities, did our large numbers make us strangers to each other? And does the competition to survive in those cities make us too busy for the people who need us most? If so, then maybe we've lost something very fundamental to our human nature.

The trip south was still dusty and hot, but at the same time amazing. We were unable to communicate with our driver so all we could do was watch the countryside as we passed through it. It was a different experience being in the carriage. We were closer to Ethiopia now. Rather than speeding by it in a large bus, we were slowly drifting through rural Ethiopian life.

Along the side of the road, the huts were small and made of dirt or stone with thatched roofs. In a place with few trees for lumber, fences were made out of cactus to keep the goats from eating the crops. While the women made fires or nursed babies, children played in the fields and front yards of the huts. As we passed, they always looked at us with astonishment. Some of the children would even chase after the carriage yelling and screaming in excitement. For a moment it felt like a Utopia, a perfect picture of human existence, despite their obvious vulnerabilities to things like war, draught, and illness.

As the sun began to set we could feel that our time here was coming to a close, although our journey was far from over. Behind us was the great and unique Ethiopian civilization. One that proved to be as exotic as it was aggravating. Ahead of us were some of the worst roadways in all of Africa, notorious for bandits, tribal fighting and broken axles on ill-equipped vehicles. But we had made our choice and were not about to turn around now.

It was starting to get dark by the time we arrived in Ethiopian Moyale, the southernmost town in the country. This would be our jumping off point into Kenya. Moyale itself is divided in half with the national border of Ethiopia and Kenya running through the middle. It now serves as the major border crossing between the two countries.

Once there, we wasted no time checking in to the nearest truck-stop/brothel hotel we could find. It wasn't as hard as one might imagine as we immediately had a young boy offer to show us to an open room. It was dark and we were tired so the assistance was much appreciated. We gave him a tip and he no doubt made a commission of the rental of the room. The price was $4 USD per night with a hole in the ground to shit in. Perfect! We were set. Out of exhaustion, we went to bed that night without eating. Although, I doubt that anything would have been open.

***

The next day we didn't stick around Ethiopian Moyale but rather made our plans to cross into the Kenyan side right away. Here, borders are usually crossed on foot so that's exactly what we did. It was a simple process of asking for directions and following the one road to the edge of town. From a distance, we could see a rickety chain-link fence that cut across the field leading up to the road. Once at the road, the chain-link fence turned into what looked like a military checkpoint where one man sat in a green army outfit holding a Kalashnikov and staring out onto the town on the other side.

"What do we do now, just walk across?" Ethan asked.

"I guess so. But I'm assuming that guy will have something to say about it."

"Where are all the cars or buses, don't people usually drive across boarders?"

"Nope, not always," I replied.

We cautiously made our way up to the man who was still sitting and staring off onto the Kenyan side of the city. He did not appear to be challenged by his job.

"Hello," I said.

The man turned around in surprise, stood up and gave us a look as if he couldn't give a shit less.

"Passport," he said.

"Sure thing," Ethan said staring at the semi-automatic weapon slung around his shoulder.

He took both our passports and went inside his booth on the side of the road. He glanced through them, looked at the photos, looked at us and pounded one hard stamp into each passport.

"Okay 60 Birr, each one," he said, as he handed them back.

We had no idea what the actual price was but it was obvious that we were in no position to negotiate, besides it was only $3 USD. Once we paid him his stated price we were free to cross into Kenya.

He opened the gate to the boarder by unhooking a long metal pole that was weighted down on the other side by a huge rock tied to a rope. This caused the metal pole to naturally rise when it was unhooked. At that point, we simply walked onto the Kenyan side and from there we would be able to determine our next move. We had arrived in a completely new country, but somehow we were still in the same city. This was now Kenyan Moyale.

CHAPTER 12
TRANSIT GAP

"What do you mean there are no buses going south? How do we get outta here? Dude! I do not want to go all the way back to Addis!" Ethan proclaimed.

We had sat down at a small outdoor eatery to have a coffee as we discussed our options, which had changed drastically after a simple border crossing.

When our orders arrived, we were presented with two cups of steaming hot water and two packets of NesCafé instant coffee. In one of the world's top coffee producing regions, something had gone very wrong with the import/export policy of coffee. It appeared they didn't keep a drop of it for themselves.

After speaking with our waiter, it seemed that we had reached a gap in the public transit system. There were no buses and no matatus going south from here...ever. The system just wasn't in place.

On the bright side, rather than just serving coffee our waiter was also a money-changer, and was able to convert our Birr and coveted US dollars into Kenyan Shillings...for a small commission of course. In Africa, people wear many hats and if he weren't changing money that day I guarantee his cousin would have been. It definitely makes for a hassle free process if you don't mind back-room money dealings.

"Relax, we'll figure it out. There has to be a way out of here...I'm sure the locals make the trip all the time."

"Yeah, but they know people!" Ethan exclaimed. "They have connections!"

"Connections? What does that matter? We have Shillings!"

"Well I'm glad you're so confident but what do we do now? There's no public transit and we're the only foreigners for miles"

"Honestly, all I want to do is find a hotel, drop off these damn bags and relax. Let's just worry about the logistics tomorrow. We've got the time," I said.

I was becoming exhausted and starting to question our choice of taking this route in the first place. We could have just gone to Thailand like normal people and drank buckets of cheap booze at all night beach parties. But instead we chose to come to one of the most inaccessible parts of east Africa just to end up getting stuck. Regardless, we had the time so there was no point in rushing through a series of all-day bus rides.

"Yeah, I can live with that. I'm in no hurry to commit to another 12-hour bus ride just yet. So where do we sleep tonight?"

"Well in my experience when all else fails, ask the guy who's been following you around all day."

From the moment we crossed the border, a young boy had been diligently following us. Over the course of the last half hour he had offered us everything from hotels to hookers, all of which we kindly ignored. But it looked as if he placed a winning bet after all, or maybe he just knew that there was no way out of Moyale that day. Either way, we were ready to buy.

"Hello my friend! Do you know of a cheap place where we can sleep tonight?"

"Yes, yes. Follow me, I will show you," he replied instantly.

"Okay, but how far away is it?"

"No problem," said the kid, as if he had a line of other customers to attend to and couldn't be bothered with stupid questions.

We followed the boy down the narrow dirt roads of Kenyan Moyale, passing the fruit stalls and open-air butcher shops, over piles of dog shit and heaps of garbage. As we paraded ourselves down the streets, we could see on-lookers in storefronts pausing their daily routines to view us in action.

"You know, you should not trust people here. They will cheat you," the boy said out of nowhere.

"Ah yes, thanks for the warning," I said, thinking that this was something people probably said right before they cheat you.

The streets were alive yet strangely still. Everyone seemed to have stopped what they were doing to watch us lug our backpacks down the street. They said nothing and their faces held no expression. Only the children were animated as they chased after us yelling out "Hello, Mister, Hello!" in an attempt to practice their English.

It wasn't long before we arrived at an unmarked wooden building; slightly unique in comparison to the typical one-story cement structures we'd been used to.

"Come," he said, as we cautiously passed the threshold into the hotel.

"This is a hotel?" said Ethan.

"Something like that."

It looked like a restaurant that hadn't been in use for years, although I'm sure food was still served nearly every day. The chairs were dusty and piled up in corners, food was sitting in display cases but all the lights were turned off and the windows were partially boarded up. The only trace of light came from a slightly cracked open door leading to a back yard.

We passed through the restaurant lobby to the back door where we stood in the middle of an open-air corridor. Hotel rooms were all around us. To our right was a group of men sitting around a small table playing what looked like poker and chain-smoking cigarettes. They acknowledged us only after we waved and smiled, but their focus quickly returned to the game.

"Wait here," said the boy as he ran around the corner.

We did as we were told.

"Hello my friends!" said a cheery voice from behind us.

There stood a shirtless man with a towel wrapped around his waist. He was holding what could only be our future room key.

"Hello, we are looking for a cheap room. Do you have anything available?"

"Yes, yes. Come, I will show you."

He led us to the second room on the left side of the corridor. It was secured with an old-fashioned latch and a padlock. The door itself was flimsy as you could see right through the cracks in between the wood. He unlocked the door and pushed it open to let us enter first. There in front of us, were two twin beds with a nightstand in between them, the standard layout. Each bed had a two-inch thick mattress and a sheet. There wasn't a lot of room but at least it was a flat place to sleep with a locking door. I looked at Ethan for his stamp of approval.

"So what do you think?"

"It looks fine to me," he replied.

We were not picky.

"Cool, how much is it per night?" I asked the man in the towel.

"For two people you will pay 300 Shillings."

Normally I would be inclined to negotiate for a better price, but something told me that there wasn't really a difference between the "tourist price" and the "local price" around these parts. Regardless, I couldn't in good conscience try to talk him down from $3 USD per night. I'm not sure a cheaper room existed anywhere. And if it did, I'm sure I didn't want to see it.

"Okay, that sounds good!"

"Okay, you pay now," said the man. "We have a toilet in back."

We dropped our bags on our beds and paid him the 300 Shillings. Ethan immediately collapsed on the bed staring at the fan spinning slowly above him as if in a trance. There were two mosquito nets, full of holes, tied up and hooked to the walls. Luckily we weren't in a Malarial zone just yet, so we could leave them alone as they would be mostly ineffective.

"I gotta take a piss. I'll be right back."

Ethan said nothing, still staring at the spinning fan.

I walked across the room by the smoky card players to the back of the hotel. The door to the bathroom was hanging halfway open. Inside, the sink drain just spilled onto the floor and the western style toilet had the toilet seat removed and propped up against the wall. Why did they insist on removing the toilet seat? A hole in the ground would make more sense at this point.

When I got back to our room I followed Ethan's lead and collapsed onto my twin bed on the other side of the room. Why was the fan so mesmerizing? And why was I so exhausted this early in the day after doing just about nothing?

We both drifted to sleep with our door wide open.

After about an hour we woke up exactly how we passed out, fully clothed, shoes on, teeth unbrushed and still covered in the filth from the day before.

"Arrrgh!!" Ethan groaned from the other side of the room.

"Food!" he yelled with the belligerence of a drunk.

I rolled to my side and slowly sat up. It was only 4PM.

"Yeah, good call. What are you in the mood for?"

"I don't know why you insist on asking me that!" Ethan said, still annoyed with his culinary experience thus far. "Let's just go find something."

After pulling ourselves together, we made our way through the hotel corridor and to the road in front. As we glared out onto the town we assessed our options on finding a meal.

"You know, I don't think we'll find many options around here," I said.

"I don't even care. As long as I can get something besides injera, I'll be good."

After a short walk around the town we realized that everything looked more or less the same. The town mostly consisted of one and two story buildings made of cement and sheet metal. Motorcycles and old cars periodically zipped past us but for the most part things were pretty slow paced. Kenyan Moyale had the classic feel of a sketchy border town where people from outlying villages would come searching for a better livelihood. Although being so remote, it lacked the constant traffic of most border towns, which gave it a slightly calmer feel.

"Ah ha! How about that place?"

"Is that a restaurant?" Ethan replied.

"Sure, look at the red plastic chairs out front! Nothing says restaurant like red plastic chairs from the Coca Cola bottling company," I assured him.

"Fair enough. Do you think it's possible to get a burger?"

"A burger? Doubtful. But on the bright side, we're now in Kenya so we might be able to get something different at least."

We cautiously made our way to the restaurant entrance and were immediately greeted by a man in brown slacks and a tucked in shirt.

"Hello my friends!"

"Hello! Do you have any food?" I said.

"Yes yes, please!" He said, as he gestured to one of the tables.

He gave each of us a menu, smiled and stood there waiting for us to decide.

"Ohh this looks great! Can I have the Chicken Sandwich?"

I looked over at Ethan, "Are we really going to go through this again?"

Disappointed, he gave up quicker this time, "Fine, just order me whatever."

"Hmmmm, what do you have?" I asked.

"We have ugali, beans, goat.....and injera!" he replies, as if injera is something we should be thrilled about.

I glanced at Ethan and he looks as if someone had just died.

"Well, I guess we'll have that then," I said with a smile on my face. "Oh, but no injera."

The restaurant was uninspiring at best, set up strictly for the purpose of dishing out food. No ambiance included. The walls were painted white and had brown stains dripping down from the ceiling, probably from rainwater. The room was filled with red plastic chair and table sets and there was a tiny counter towards the far back wall.

It couldn't have been more than five minutes when the waiter came back with a small bowl of goat meat and a large plate of injera. Ethan just looked at me.

"I guess he misunderstood the order," I said in an attempt to be upbeat.

"I guess."

"Hey don't worry. Wait for the ugali, you'll love the ugali!"

"Yeah?"

"Haha no, absolutely not! But it's not injera."

"Hey! Isn't that the kid from this morning?" Ethan interrupted.

"Yeah, that's him! Hey we should ask him if there is a bus heading south?

"Sure, why not."

I got up out of my red plastic chair and briskly walked over to flag the kid down. Luckily he noticed me pretty quick; of course in this town I was pretty noticeable.

"My friend, hello! How are you?" he asked cheerfully.

"Ohh hello, I'm good."

"How is your hotel?"

"Very good, thank you. I have a quick question for you. Do you know if there is a bus to Marsabit or Lake Turkana from here, or anywhere south?"

"No," he smiles and shakes his head.

"How about a matatu?"

"No," he smiles and shakes his head again.

It always helps to ask the same question to multiple people, as you will get multiple answers, often times conflicting with each other. But not this time.

"Oh, well, do you know how we can get there?"

"Yes, you must go by freight truck."

"Freight truck? When does that leave?"

The boy proceeded to explain to me the standard process of heading south from Kenyan Moyale. And although William had mentioned that traveling along these roads was difficult due to shoddy infrastructure and frequent hijackings, I guess I didn't fully grasp the situation.

After thanking the kid I made my way back to the red plastic chairs at the restaurant where Ethan was just staring at a plate of ugali in disbelief.

"What the hell is this stuff?" Ethan exclaimed.

"Its ugali, basically it's cornmeal all clumped together into one solid white lump. Think of it as the injera of Kenya…it's their staple carbohydrate."

"That just makes me sad."

"So you tried it?" I asked.

"Yeah, I tried it. It's not good."

"No, but its much better with beans," I said optimistically.

"I'm sure it is. So what's the plan? How do we get out of this town?"

"Well, apparently we can't leave today. No surprise there. But we can probably leave tomorrow morning."

"Probably. What do you mean probably? What time does our ride leave?"

"Well, basically, we're gonna have to hitchhike

out....kind of."

With a serious face, he just looked at me.

"Okay, so let me tell you what I know...which isn't much. Basically we need to be at the town center at 9AM tomorrow morning to catch a freight truck south to the town of Marsabit. They gather up everyone who wants to go and leave as a group."

"Well that doesn't sound too complicated. How much is it?"

"He said it was 500 Shillings each."

"Nice, so what do we do until then?"

"I think there's only one thing we can do....shower up and go to the local pub."

"Well I like the pub idea, but showering?? Just skip it!" Ethan said eager to get the party started.

"Dude I can't, I need to wash off this filth!"

"I'm sorry to break this to you but all the soap and water in the world won't clean your kind of filth," Ethan assured me.

"You're a funny guy."

We finished our ugali and beans, paid our bill and made our way back to the hotel. While Ethan assumed his position of lying on the bed and staring at the fan, I left in search of the shower. Luckily I knew exactly where to find the owner; shirtless, in the main courtyard, playing cards with his buddies.

"Ah Hello! Excuse me but I was wondering if you had a shower?"

"Ahh yes, yes. Come!"

He wasted no time in calling for assistance, and after a string of incomprehensible shoutings a young boy came running up to us ready to assist. He was short and very skinny and judging by the way he was treated I had to guess that he was an employee rather than family.

"Okay, go! You can follow this boy."

"Oh, okay. Thanks a lot!"

He led and I followed as we walked all the way to the

back of the hotel, past the rooms and up a set of cement stairs that took us to an open air landing overlooking the small African town. There was a row of doors that lined the wall on one side and a large pile of old chairs that filled a significant portion of the opposite corner. The cement walls were only raised two feet from the floor and still had the rusted rebar poking out from the top as if they had suddenly stopped construction without finishing the final touches.

As I stood there confused, the boy began to drag a large piece of sheet metal across the floor. In doing so, he uncovered what appeared to be a very dark and very deep hole. He lowered a large bucket tied with a rope slowly down the hole. Within moments he pulled the bucket back out, this time full of murky well water. He then detached it from the rope and lugged it over to a small room at the corner of the roof, the last door in the line.

"Here, you shower here," he said as he handed me a small cup for bucket-bathing.

"Ah okay, thank you."

The room was four feet by four feet. There was no lighting and no plumbing aside from a small hole in the corner of the floor to let the water drain. The water in the bucket was a nice golden brown. What I wasn't sure of was whether the water's color was a result of dirt or rust. I chose to believe that it was just dirt because for some reason I felt that showering with rust would have been worse. Regardless, I knew my way around a bucket-bath, although this was my first one using well water. Still, I was in no position to complain.

I latched the rickety wooden door and undressed. I squatted down and began the "bucket bathing process"...rinse, lather and rinse again. This was how the majority of the worlds' people bathed themselves but for me, in my life, it was the exception. It was times like these where I realized that a nice hot shower is one of the finest things in life.

When I arrived back at the room Ethan was asleep on his bed, laying on his back, limbs stretched out like a giant X.

"Wake up! Go shower you mangy mongrel!"

I threw my damp towel on his face.

"Ahh, asshole!" he replied.

"So where's this shower at?"

"It's at the top of the stairs, last room in the back."

"Cool, how is it?"

"It's, eh...meager."

"Ohh great! I'm not going to get hepatitis C from this little experience, am I?" he said as if he was half upset and half getting used to it.

"I'd say you've got about a 50/50 chance."

"Well, here's to rolling the dice!" he said as he walked out of the room with his soap and travelers towel in hand.

"Oh hey! You'll need to tell the kid that you need a bucket of water for the shower."

"What? I can't just fill it myself?"

"There's no faucet."

"So where do we get the water from?"

"Just ask the kid, you'll see."

The look on his face was one of disappointment and defeat. He turned and walked out without saying another word.

I fell back onto my bed and picked up where Ethan left off, staring at the spinning fan above. It was nice to have a moment of silent contemplation. As I lay there zoning out, I remembered the manila envelope in my bag. The unfinished book my dad started but never completed. I guess books are like that. Life gets in the way.

I rolled over, unzipped the top pouch of my backpack and pulled out the envelope. I reached for the next chapter in the sequence and prepared to settle in for a good read while Ethan finished his shower. It was titled "Let's Make a Deal".

CHAPTER 13
LET'S MAKE A DEAL!

Dad loved to buy, sell, and trade vehicles. It didn't matter what the vehicle was or even if he had any possible use for the vehicle. If a trade or favorable purchase could be made, Dad was going to get that vehicle. If the vehicle cost a hundred and Dad could sell it for a hundred and ten, that was great; if he could only sell it for ninety, well that was okay too. It wasn't if money was made or lost in any given transaction, it was the challenge of the deal.

My first personal memory of Dad and his vehicle deals was back in my grade school years. It wasn't uncommon to see a wide variety and ever-changing inventory of cars, trucks, trailers, and all possible combinations thereof, in our back yard. Dad would buy, trade, or somehow obtain those vehicles, and line them up, six or eight or ten in a row and drive a different one every day, hoping to sell or trade a different one every day. The cars were old Datsons, and Nashes, and Studebakers, and Cadillacs and many were, surprisingly, quite fancy even for their age.

Dad was able to keep his inventory of cars constantly increasing and decreasing and changing because of the market he cultivated with all us kids, his nieces and nephews, and, above all, his truck drivers. Many of those drivers were offered, and accepted, a car in lieu of wages and all of us kids were allowed to use the cars, as available, for our own transportation into town. As we became older and a bit more discerning on what we drove, we used his cars as trade-ins with the car dealers in town.

Around 1966, when I was a freshman in high school, I had my first experience with Dad in negotiating a purchase of a car. Dad had allowed me, as well as all us kids, to get a driver's license at a young age so we could, allegedly arrange our own transportation into town. We all knew, however, that his real motive in letting us enter the driving world was to enlarge his market for his used cars. However in that year of 1966 I caught my Dad at a very awkward time; I needed a car and he had none available which met my strict specifications. Actually my specifications were not that strict; the car had to run, period. So Dad and I went to see his favorite car dealer in Bismarck, Honest Harry of Honest Harry's Used and New Cars.

Dad told me to pick out the car I wanted and not worry about the price; we would apparently disregard any asking price and beat poor Honest Harry into submission with some combination of cash and trade. I picked out a 1955 Studebaker Commander, sticker price at $130 (remember this was in 1966). The details of the negotiations, after all these years are faint but I recall that Dad was firm that we would take the car for $50 (cash, not financed) with Harry also getting an option for a trade on some future unknown and unnamed vehicle at some later date. Apparently Honest Harry had dealt with Dad before because a promise of some future trade didn't seem to excite him. We started looking at that car in the morning and kept poor Harry talking about that car until late in the afternoon. After a number of offers and counteroffers, we ultimately bought that Studebaker for $65 and a box of apples.

That $65 Studebaker was worth a $1,000 to me in terms of understanding how to negotiate. Dad's laws of negotiation are; take your time, and the time of the salesman (this makes the poor salesman have a heavy investment of time in you and encourages him to close some type of deal with you to profit from that investment); create a wide gap between the asking price and the first offer (it's easy to judge the value of an item if the salesman continues to negotiate even with a low offer on the table); and always offer something in trade. A $65 bill and a box of apples is better than just $65.

Throughout the rest of my life, whenever I felt the urge to buy a car I took Dad along to act as chief negotiator. Because many of the car dealers knew and liked my Dad, it often seemed that they were willing to make outlandish trades with him.

Many years after that first car when I was preparing to purchase a new pickup from a local dealer in Bismarck, I took Dad in with me to put the final polishing touches on my deal. The conversation my Dad had is clear in my mind:

Unsuspecting Salesman Jim, meeting and shaking hands with Dad: "And you are?"

Dad: "Homer Royse."

Salesman Jim: "Um, your name sounds familiar." To me, "Well Ken, are we ready to mark this vehicle with a big 'S'?"

Supposedly "S" stood for either sucker or sale.

Dad, taking out a pen and making notes on the back of an envelope: "You bet we're ready but we're not sure you're ready. What was that total price again?"

Salesman Jim: "We're at the sales price of $5,100 after the trade for Ken's pickup."

Dad, agreeable but perplexed: "Okay, then what is the price after the trade-in?"

Salesman Jim: "Ah, $5,100. The $5,100 is after the trade-in of Ken's pickup."

At this my Dad is shocked. He cannot believe Jim wants $5,100 after the trade, he shakes his head, he adds and subtracts various numbers on his envelope and it becomes clear that the trade in offered by Jim makes him very sad. It sure would have been nice to be able to get that new vehicle and mark it with an "S".

Jim, seeing how distressed this is making my Dad: "Well, maybe we can talk a little about that price but it's really close to rock bottom."

This seems to satisfy Dad and he shifts gears, "When did you want to schedule fixing that front window of the new pickup?"

"Windshield?"

"Well yeah, the windshield has a crack. If Ken buys this pickup I may want to borrow it and I can't be driving anything with a crack in the windshield."

"Um, yeah. Just a minute, let me check with my manager."

Now Jim is confused. What crack? What price did we agree on? What happened to his sure sale?

Salesman Jim returns and he is rejuvenated after talking to his manager. Fix the windshield? No problem. A little more, but just a little, for the trade-in? No problem. But, doing those items, can he mark his pickup with an "S"? Salesman Jim feels good, his sure sale has returned.

But Dad has just started his negotiations. Did Jim know that the new pickup didn't have an engine block heater? Did he know the heater fan makes a funny noise? And worse of all there is a concern with the scratches in the box of the new pickup; after all, as Dad reminds Jim, "I'll want to borrow this pickup from Ken and I can't drive a pickup with scratches in it". While Dad is explaining to Jim his concern with these defects I have to fight a laugh. I've seen Dad use the hood of his car to haul truck tires and tools around the yard and into town, and it had long been family knowledge that Dad believes vehicles have to be well broke in to show them who the boss is.

Now poor Salesman Jim is confused. He excuses himself, again, to confer with his Manager. He's mumbling about scratches in the box as he walks away.

When he returns, my Dad is apparently feeling sorry for Jim, and for all the trouble and time the transaction has begun to take and so offers a reasonable compromise to the poor fellow. Dad is nothing if not fair.

Dad, "I think to keep this deal moving we're going to have to have you take another vehicle in trade along with Ken's pickup."

Salesman Jim, "Another trade?"

Now the trap is set. All negotiations and discussions up to this time mean nothing. I know, but poor Jim has no idea, what lies ahead.

"Well," Dad begins. "We think that we could go with your deal on your pickup but you should take one more vehicle in on trade to bring the total price down to $4,100. We've got a couple of vehicles you could look at and take your choice."

Poor unsuspecting Salesman Jim: "Um, that may be possible...what have you got?"

Now Dad goes into a listing and description of a variety of vehicles he currently has in his trading stock. They include a variety of older model cars including a 1973 Datsun, a 1974 Oldsmobile, several 1972 to 1975 Buicks, and a 1968 International Pickup. All such vehicles range from 15 to 18 years old.

Salesman Jim only looks at my Dad. He can't believe he has heard correctly. Did he really hear that we wanted to trade in an old car; was this just a bad dream? He looks at me but he sees that I'm serious about this too.

Dad continues, "And we also got a nice 1961 school bus that has been made into a camper, and we got a 1962 van that's fixed up as a contractors wagon, and we got a real nice, a little rough, 1977 Chevy van."

In the total listing of possible trade-in vehicles, Dad has used the phrase "real nice" to describe only the 1977 van, so that to me, obviously, is my clue as to which one Jim is going to end up getting.

Salesman Jim: "Uh, how many miles on the 77 van?"

Dad: "Oh, I don't know, we haven't had it very long...we don't drive it too much."

Jim, making a note, "Well let's say it has 100,000 miles

on it."

Dad, "Well, as long as we're guessing, let's say 50,000."

After some prolonged discussion and several trips to confer with his manager Salesman Jim agrees to come out and drive the van back to the shop for an appraisal. He is now in the process of putting his other foot in Dad's trap.

As a personal aside here, people often ask me why neither I, nor any of us kids hunt or fish. Stalking, shooting and dragging a deer out of the woods doesn't compare to the thrill of cornering a car salesman. And you don't have to buy a license.

When we get to Dad's yard to pick up the van, Salesman Jim now learns the definition of "a little rough". The van has no mirrors, the body is badly rusted, the back seats are missing, there is no gas or brake pedal, nor is there a drivers side window or interior heater. Jim is stunned, he can't believe we want $1,000 trade in value on this van; he can't believe he has to take the vehicle back to his manager for an appraisal. He can't believe he wore his new suit on this day and now he has to drive this vehicle back, through town, while sitting on an orange crate.

We start the van up for Jim, and now Dad is stunned. The van wasn't supposed to start that easy. Dad has forgotten to take the good battery out of the van and put in a substitute scrap battery.

As I drive back to Bismarck, I can see that Salesman Jim is following behind me in the '77 van. There is no window on the driver's side, and there is no interior heater. The wind is blowing (this is late fall and very cold) and Jim is driving hunched over, shivering, and with blue lips. I can see him repeating the whole trip "This is a piece of junk, this is a piece of junk, this is a piece of junk."

But, junk or not, Dad ultimately got that dealer to allow us $900 on that old van, and we got the windshield fixed, the new box liner, and a new engine block heater on the new pickup we bought. And Salesman Jim got a story to tell his little children on Halloween night. You kids be good, or mean old Homer Royse will getcha!

CHAPTER 14
TUSKER COUNTRY

"I think we've reached a new low!" Ethan proclaimed as he pushed the room door open and broke my concentration.

"What's the problem?" I said, fully knowing that he was complaining about the shower situation.

"I think it's clear that you use the word "shower" far too loosely."

"Hahaha! So you're saying you didn't enjoy yourself?"

"Actually it was fine, I'm just not sure if I'm cleaner now or before I took the shower."

"Na, you're cleaner. You smelled like shit before, now you just smell like stale well water. It was a much needed improvement."

"Well, that's excellent!" he replied.

As Ethan got dressed, I put the loose papers back into the tan envelope without mentioning a word about the story I had just read. Ethan was a big Reggae fan so he promptly plugged his iPod into his tiny travel speakers and turned on "Stir it Up" by Bob Marley. Somehow the song felt appropriate despite our surroundings. As the light from the setting sun began to stream into the room through the holes in the curtains, I laid there staring at the fan twirling above as I thought about what I had just read, our trip so far and the road that lay ahead of us.

At this point there was nothing pressing to do until morning when we would hopefully be able to catch the freight trucks south. So we proceeded to do what any self-respecting backpackers would do, which is sample the local brew.

Once again we found ourselves standing in front of our hotel staring out onto the deserted dirt road. It was 7PM and the town was nearly shut down. Only a few people shuffled around in the darkness, only a few shops remained open and only a few small fires continued to burn as families began to wind down for the night. Despite our empty surroundings, it wasn't long before we came across the local watering hole. Some things are the same everywhere and one of those things is that every small town everywhere in the world has a bar.

The bar was called "Jambo House" and on the wall outside it indicated that they served food and beer. It was a small non-descript cement structure but an indication of what they sold was enough for us. As we crossed the entrance of the establishment and made our way to the bar, every head began to turn our way. Like an old western movie where a stranger walks into the bar and everything stops for a moment, we descended upon their local pub. This wasn't a town that saw a lot of foreigners and we were as out of place as you could get. We approached the bartender timidly but her smiling face was reassuring.

"Hello my friends! What will it be?"

"Hmmm, St. George?" Ethan looked over as if it was an obvious choice.

"Ah ah ah, not so fast. We're in Tusker country now!"

"What the hell is that?"

"It's Kenyan beer, of course! I saw it advertised on the side of a store front."

"I don't know how you noticed that."

"I always pick up on a country's main brew when I arrive. It's important."

He looked at me like I was an idiot, "You should have picked up on the lack of public transit here instead."

"I'm not sure that I appreciate your tone," I said

jokingly.

"Can we have two Tuskers please?" Ethan said to the bar tender.

"Yes, of course!" She said with a smile.

This particular place consisted of a long bar built across the left wall of the room and booths across the right side. In the middle were a number of tables and chairs scattered around an open-air floor. In back was the kitchen. And at the center of everything was a single large tree that made an otherwise unremarkable place something unique. We grabbed our drinks and sat down at a table underneath the tree. The faces surrounding us slowly began to turn away as we gradually became less interesting.

However, within moments a man walked over to our table to welcome us to the bar. He was tall and thin, clean-shaven and with short black hair. His face was long and he spoke loudly with swooping had gestures.

"My friends, hello!" he said with a huge smile. "What brings you both to Moyale?"

"Hello!" Ethan replied. "We're just passing through on a backpacking trip."

"So just traveling? Why?" the man seemed puzzled.

Confused, Ethan answered back, "Yeah, just traveling...for fun."

The man's face changed instantly from confusion to amusement, "Hahaha! You muzungus are very funny! Always going places for no reason. Where are your wives and children? Are they with you?"

"Muzungu" is a common term in east Africa that simply means "white person". It's not meant to be derogatory in any way, it's simply a term that addresses you as what you are...a white person.

"No," I said. "We are not married and don't have any kids."

His previous look of amusement had now changed to sadness after hearing this recent news, "Oh I am sorry to hear that, but I am sure that your luck will change one day.

So, will you be doing anything while you are here, working or volunteering?"

"No, just passing through," I replied, feeling a little ashamed.

"Oh I see. Well, that is a smart choice!"

"Really…why is that?" I said, surprised.

"Because, my friends! You do not need to save Africa. The United Nations has been trying to do that for years…hahaha! And we surely don't need you to come here and take our jobs…hahaha!"

"So you don't want the volunteers to come over?"

"It is not necessary."

"But doesn't it help if people donate time or money to Africa? " I replied, slightly confused.

"Well, many muzungus come to Africa and think they can change it for us, as if we can do nothing for ourselves. But this is Africa! This is our place and we will do the work that needs to be done. Have you seen the UN everywhere?"

"Yes, their white 4x4's are all over the place," I said, despite fearing that we were heading toward a political discussion that could last all night.

"Yes, they are. And they are the wealthiest people in Africa. The UN workers will become rich while the villagers stay poor. You see, they do not serve the people. They only serve themselves. Truly fortunate is the man who finds employment with the United Nations….Hahaha!"

"Oh, I didn't realize. But don't they help people who need it? Doesn't some of the UN's work or other volunteers benefit Africa?" I replied.

"Hmm, well it doesn't hurt Africa. But it is mostly for the people doing the work. The people who come to Africa to see and learn, they will benefit from that experience. The UN worker who can better provide for his family will have a better life. So, overall it is a good thing for them. For us, it is only okay."

"Some good must come of it…for Africa?" I said, as I tried to remember some of the failed programs that were designed to "save Africa".

"Yes, yes of course! Sometimes it is good, but most of the time nothing changes. This is just my opinion of course."

Like a chameleon, his mood switched back to joyful as he attempted to bring the conversation to a conclusion, "Okay, my friends…please enjoy Africa! I must get back to my family."

"Okay, sounds good. Nice to meet you!" Ethan replied.

After a short pause, long enough to take about one sip of beer, Ethan announced triumphantly, "See, I told you volunteering was a waste of time!"

"Well, I'm happy you've found validation for your apathy toward mankind," I said sarcastically.

It was a strange thing to hear. In the States, we're always taught the benefits of volunteer work. I always assumed we needed to do much more to help those in need. But we had found a person who looked at it differently. To him, it was less about helping people than it was about foreigners blindly throwing money at a problem. Maybe he was right. Maybe he had just come across a lot of failed programs. Regardless, it was an interesting point of view. And one that really had me questioning mine. I just wasn't quite ready to give up on the benefits of volunteerism in Africa.

"So I have to ask, why on earth do you travel to places like this? It seems so irrational," Ethan asked, in what may have been his first serious question of the trip.

"Irrational?" I exclaimed. "I see it as more of an adventure."

"Okay, I guess so. But still, normal people don't just buy plane tickets to Africa and wander around with no plan. Why not just go to a beach and get wasted for two weeks?"

"Okay, okay, I see where you're going with this. I guess

I think that doing something unique and exciting is a reward in itself…even if it's not always comfortable. And on top of that, when you can share that experience with someone else it becomes even more valuable. It's actually funny that you bring it up, because while you were in the shower I was reading these stories that Dad gave me about his childhood with grandpa and it got me thinking….

"Wait, what!" he interrupted.

"Before I left Dad gave me an envelope full of stories that he had written about grandpa. He said he was planning on writing a book but never got around to finishing it.

"Okay," Ethan was losing interest.

"Anyway, I think you should read these!"

"Dude, I've been home for Christmas every year. I've heard them all. Trust me."

"And how would you know that?" I replied.

"Fine, do you have them with you? Read me one. I could use something more entertaining than this conversation anyway, and it better not be boring! I'd hate to have to drink myself into a stupor the night before our big journey south."

"We both knew you were going to do that anyway," I said sarcastically.

"Not if you can keep my attention."

From my small bag I pulled out the next story in the sequence. It was titled "Shark, for Sale or Rent". I knew this one just had to keep his attention.

CHAPTER 15
SHARK, FOR SALE OR RENT

In and around 1980-81, Dad came home from one of his many road trips with the biggest trade of his life; this was a trade to top all other trades; this was a trade from which legends are made.

Dad brought home a 17 1/2 foot great white shark, frozen and on display in a refrigerated semi-van.

On the outside of the van, on both sides, were large painted pictures of a great white shark, with mouth wide open and glaring out at the world. The pictures were captioned:

"Come See The Deadliest Beast Of The Seven Seas."
"17 ½ Foot Great White Shark"

...and in smaller letters.

"Caught off the Coast of California."
"Not Suitable For Small Children or the Faint of Heart."
"Admission Just $ .50"

...and in the smallest letters.

"Kids under 12...$0.25"

The van holding the shark was kept cold by means of an electrical refrigeration unit mounted at the front. People wanting to see the shark entered on a set of fold down steps off the back of the trailer and passed by a ticket booth ("Tickets $ .50, Please keep Hands In Pockets") and into a room divided from the outside by a hanging curtain.

There, mounted and glaring behind a glass wall, and very cold and frozen, was the great white shark. His eyes and mouth were propped open toward the audience in a menacing position and his rows of sharp triangular teeth were prominently displayed. He clearly had been, at least at one time, the King of the Sea.

It was an impressive display; well worth the cost of admission. But it was also fairly obvious that this old shark had long been a fish out of water. He may have been a 17 1/2 foot length at one time, but time (and a faulty refrigeration unit) had taken a toll on him. He had been frozen and thawed and frozen and thawed so many times that he looked to be only about 12 to 14 feet long and it was almost possible to count each of his ribs and bones.

But regardless if that shark was 14 feet or 17 feet in length he was still the biggest show in town.

When Dad pulled that shark into the yard he became an instant local celebrity. The area newspapers came out and took pictures and ran local interest stories. This was a big news story for Mandan-Bismarck; forget about the local fireman who had just saved three kids and a dog from a burning house, forget about the lady in Wishek who had a 60 pound zucchini, Homer Royse had a great white shark in his yard.

Mom best phrased the question on everyone's mind to Dad, "Homer are you crazy? What are you going to do with a frozen shark?"

To which Dad would reply, "Why, they're a lot of things to do with the shark. We'll use it to sell produce, we'll rent it out to supermarkets to have grand openings, maybe we'll just cut him up and have fish sandwiches all winter." As always with Dad, there were all sorts of logical reasons for his decisions.

At the time Dad brought old "Sharky" into the yard and into his business, it was the fall of the year and the pumpkin and Halloween season was close. So Dad figured he'd put the fish right to work to help entice customers to the place to improve pumpkin sales. It made sense to Dad; pumpkins and sharks, a natural combination. Dad pulled the shark around front and ran local ads in the papers:

"See the Great White Shark at Royse's Produce."
"Limited Time Only."
"Buy a Pumpkin and Get Free Admission."

Of course, Dad was a born promoter and there wasn't any product or item, no matter how unique (not even a shark in the middle of North Dakota), that he wouldn't try to find some way to make it appear a bit more interesting. After some thought, he hit upon an idea for adding another dimension to make Old Sharky seem a bit more menacing. His thought was to hire a ticket salesman to handle the tickets and the crowds; and if this ticket salesman happened to be missing an arm, or a leg, well that was okay; and if the one-armed or one-legged ticket salesman was a bit of a story teller (especially fish stories), so much the better.

But search as he would, no one-armed or one-legged fish story telling ticket salesman could be found. So Old Sharky was put on display to the general public without the benefit of the history and adventures of his fish life being told with each ticket sold.

The shark business was good that fall and people came from all parts of the area to see the shark and buy a pumpkin. Those who didn't really want to buy a pumpkin were allowed to see Old Sharky anyway at no cost just, as my Dad figured, as a general service to the public.

Dad and his shark became fairly well known. Every time Dad went out to eat, some waitress or patron of the cafe would always say "Homer, try the fish today" and

Dad would always reply "No thanks, got plenty of fish at home".

Old Sharky wintered fairly well that year in his van out back behind the house. Occasionally, on warmer winter days we could smell Sharky thawing and shrinking and on a few occasions we had to chase away neighborhood cats from their continuous ongoing investigation of that van.

Although when we looked at that old shriveled up fish we saw nothing more than a curiosity item and occasional sales tool for selling produce, Dad saw a business opportunity of endless proportions. Dad believed there were perhaps no businesses that could not benefit by having a shark display to draw in the general public. So with that belief, Dad began negotiating the leasing of the shark. Now it no longer was a frozen shark on display; now, on advise of attorney son Alex, it was an "exhibit".

And because it was now an "exhibit" rather than just a shark, Dad figured it was necessary to put insurance on that business asset. Dad found that North Dakota is a funny place to be a business visionary; it was possible to insure cows and chickens and wheat fields and corn rows, but not possible to find a carrier for a great white shark, even if that great white was called an "exhibit". Dad eventually was able to put coverage on the shark by a policy through Lloyds of London (London, England). Very possibly Dad was their only frozen shark account.

That spring Dad sent Sharky out on what was envisioned to be the first of many road jobs. Dad made arrangements for Old Sharky to be the featured attraction at a car dealers grand spring sale in some small town in Idaho. Dad had visions that this could lead to an even wider market; Sharky could be used at fairs and carnivals, for rodeos, and for a tourist attraction. Dad even thought a new law firm opening in town might benefit from Old Sharky during their official opening but they apparently were not interested.

So Old Sharky started west to Idaho and to a car dealer

grand opening. But Lady Fate is a funny thing. Perhaps it was just ordained that Old Sharky's career as a parking lot attraction was not to be, or perhaps, as we all thought, it was destined that Dad's fame and notoriety with Old Sharky was to be more widespread than just within the confines of the Bismarck-Mandan area.

At any rate, when Dad's driver got to western North Dakota he decided, for some reason, perhaps to surprise relatives, to take a detour north through Williston, North Dakota. Williston is off the normal route to Idaho, and to get there the driver would be off the interstate and on a two lane state highway through the badlands of North Dakota. The Dakota badlands are areas of deep ravines and steep side slopes. Although the highway is fairly good and wide, the area is not one that you would want to break down in or have to pull off the road for any reason.

But Homer Royse's Law of Trucking was holding true to form, "Never Break Down in the Day Time, Always At Night; Never Break Down On a Flat Highway, Always On a Hill; Never Break Down In Town, Always In the Middle of Nowhere". So naturally the driver of the van with Old Sharky broke down, in the middle of the night, in the middle of the steep hills of the badlands, and a good ten miles from the nearest town.

That nearest town was Wadford City and the night was mild so Dad's driver figured he may as well leave the truck and walk into town and get help; he wasn't particularly worried about any area farmer coming out and stealing Old Sharky while he was gone.

Sometime later the driver returned with a tow truck. The tow truck driver was excited; he was going to tow a frozen shark. This was big news in Wadford City; so much so that the tow truck driver had called his girlfriend to come along and be part of history.

But where was that shark trailer? There was no sign of a truck, a trailer, or of Old Sharky. Then Dad's driver saw what had happened. Way down in the bottom of a ravine, tipped on its side, was the van holding Old Sharky. The front of the van had been torn off and the shark was hanging half in and half out.

When the driver called Dad early that morning with the news, Dad told him not to do anything, he'd be coming right out. Dad called me and wanted me to go with him and of course I was concerned. At three in the morning I wasn't thinking as clearly as I should have been so I agreed to go. In my mind I questioned: Was there much damage? Could Old Sharky be saved? Who had a grudge against our shark?

But Dad had other concerns on his mind as I found out when we got there. After picking up the driver of the truck we went to the accident site for a first hand investigation. Dad and the driver scrambled down that ravine and starting hooking hoisting ropes and harnesses on the shark, supposedly (I thought) to put him back into the van. But Dad's theory was different; he didn't want the shark in the van, he wanted that shark out of the van.

Dad's thought process was simple, "I'm not going to spend the next year arguing with some insurance adjuster about the value of partial damage to that shark; that shark is either completely undamaged or he's going to be completely damaged". And in that warm spring air, it wasn't going to take but a few hours for Old Sharky to be completely damaged.

News of the damaged shark traveled fast. Son Alex called in and said he had been driving to work in his office in San Francisco that morning and something on the Paul Harvey newscast caught his ear. Paul Harvey had used the words "great white shark" and "North Dakota" in the same sentence and Alex just knew it had to involve Dad.

The area newspaper people picked up on and followed the story. They all wanted to know; What was the extent of the damage? Would Dad find a way to replace the shark? And to all of these questions, Dad would just shake his head and say "We really don't know. The damage was pretty bad. We're hoping the insurance company can replace the exhibit, we don't want any money settlement on this."

The insurance company was at a complete loss on how to resolve the issue. They would offer Dad some amount of cash settlement to resolve the loss and Dad would always decline, wanting instead for the exhibit to just be either fixed or replaced. It didn't take long for the insurance company to realize that the cost of locating, catching, freezing, and displaying a great white shark was something they probably didn't want to be involved in, so the settlement offer kept growing. And all during this time, Dad was reminding them that, according to the policy, the shark exhibit was really their property at that time and he was only storing it for them. Before too long it dawned on the insurance company that if they weren't careful they would have to deal with a big storage bill as well as the cost of settling on the shark.

And beyond that, well if Dad had to dispose of Old Sharky there was no telling what the funeral bill might run.

For the rest of that summer and into the fall Old Sharky sat in his wrecked van in the back of Dad's yard. The van had been boarded up and sealed to keep cats and other animals from feasting on Old Sharky and Dad had long since quit keeping the shark frozen. As that shark thawed all that summer we all kept hearing customers at the fruit stand asking what was that smell that was something like fish? Dad told them it probably came from Faulkners Market down the road.

Ultimately Dad and the insurance company came to an agreement on the value of Old Sharky, the van, and the storage bill. On the day that settlement was reached, Dad hooked up to that old exhibit van and pulled it all out to the Mandan landfill. There the landfill operator opened a big hole and Old Sharky was pushed in, van and all and now serves as landfill under a housing development area for the City.

Dad was right when he brought that shark into the yard the year before. It was a good business deal; no, he wasn't crazy; and you bet, he'd buy another one if he could only find one. For the next one though he would definitely find a one-armed man to help promote it.

CHAPTER 16
THE CONVOY

As the sun began to rise over Kenyan Moyale the town awoke to the slow accumulation of freight trucks congregating in the town's central square. They were forming a convoy to move south to the small town of Marsabit, located a little further down the road in what was still considered northern Kenya. Once in Marsabit, we'd have more options as to which route to take next. Northern Kenya is quite different from the rest of Kenya. So much so that the locals have affectionately nicknamed it "The Wild West" due to its lack of transport, lawlessness and remote location. I became fully aware of this fact as the convoy began to form.

"Hello my friends!" a voice said from behind us. "Do you travel today?"

"Hello, yes we want to take the truck to Marsabit."

"Okay yes, you will wait here. Please stay here."

"Okay, great! Hey, I have a question for you. Why do we wait for so many trucks before leaving?" I asked the man organizing the trucks.

"Ohh we must wait!" he said with complete seriousness. "These roads have many bandits who have guns. If you travel alone it is not safe. But when we travel in large groups they are too scared to hijack and we can get through no problem. They used to kill everyone they caught, but now they only steal. It is much better now." He finished his statement with a big smile.

"Oh, well that's good." I wasn't sure exactly how to respond, but that's what came out.

There we waited on the side of the dirt road, me with a bottle of water and Ethan munching on a package of "biscuits" that he had purchased from a corner store. They were basically cheap sugar cookies like the kind you might find at a 99-cent store. But as tasteless as they were, it's always a good idea to have something to eat on these long journeys. You never know when they'll be stopping for lunch. Unfortunately Ethan was going through them pretty quick.

At this point my first concern was having a hijack-free day in Africa. My second concern was finding food. I won't lie, food was a close second. It was also the only thing I had any control over. Unfortunately there was no food in sight and we were given specific instructions to wait where we were. As a result, there was only one thing left to do...plug in and tune out. I grabbed my iPod, cranked up my favorite travel band and continued to stare off into the distance. The dusty little town became my personal hard rock music video, although the lyrics didn't really match the setting.

We sat there for what must have been two hours as the freight trucks slowly lined up in a row awaiting their launch south. As each truck pulled up to the queue it was swarmed by groups of men who would yell and direct people to where they should sit. Once each truck was in place, it would turn off its engine and await further instructions.

Periodically one of us would go in search of food, always returning with one of the same three things; biscuits, bananas, or goat meat on a stick. The goat meat was the obvious winner.

From our little area on the side of the road underneath the acacia tree we were finally called to board the freight truck. A man with no distinguishing marks as an authority figure quickly walked up to us and directed us to our place in the back of truck.

"My friends, come, come! We are leaving very soon!"

"Oh okay, great! Let's go," I turned to face Ethan and he was already up with his backpack on. I think he was tired of waiting.

The man led us to the back of the truck where we were able to climb up along the outside of the truck's frame and enter from the top. The roof of the truck was just a metal frame partially covered with a green tarp. As we dropped down we landed on a massive pile of rock-hard bagged beans. Our seats were at the front right side of the truck. As we situated ourselves into our corner we noticed a dozen expressionless faces staring back at us. These were our new travel buddies, our road trip crew. And now, we were assembled and ready make the journey south.

Only half of the truck's roof was covered with the thick green tarp. The other half had been pulled back and tied down on the sides, which allowed the brutal African sun to pour in through the uncovered portion of the vehicle. To make it worse, the heat from the sun was being trapped inside the vehicle by the covered portion of the green tarp, which happened to be where we were sitting. But for some reason Ethan and I were the only people covered in sweat. It was clear that we were out of our element.

After another 20 minutes or so in our sweltering hotbox we began to hear shouting coming from outside the truck. The shouting was then followed by the sweet sound of ignition as the trucks began to start their engines.

"Oh thank the lord!" I said, knowing that the breeze would cool down the truck. "I think we're about to leave."

"Good." Ethan replied in an agitated tone.

I grabbed my black bandana and wiped the dripping sweat from my face. I needed to see what was happening outside. Standing on my section of the bean pile I could peer out on the town around us. With my head poking out of the back of the truck I could see the miraculous result of all the shouting and yelling that had taken place over the course of the morning. There before me was a convoy of ten large green freight trucks lined up in an organized row, engines roaring and ready to move like a military awaiting their command. It may take a lot longer to get things done in Africa but it sure as hell still gets done.

In front of us I could see the first truck begin to pull out, then the second, then ours. As we moved forward with the wind on my face my mood instantly changed from being completely pissed off to calm and tranquil. A sense of freedom came over me as we began to speed down the dirt road and out of a town that we hoped we wouldn't have to see again.

The town of Moyale quickly disappeared behind us to be replaced by endless seas savanna dotted with acacia trees. We were now traveling through the Great Rift Valley of northern Kenya. To our west was Lake Turkana, home to some of Africa's more traditional tribes and in between them and us were the bandits we were trying to avoid. The sun was hot, the road was pot-holed and the beans were uncomfortable but I didn't care. We were officially on the road again, and that was the feeling I loved.

As I sat back down, I glanced around the back of the truck and took notice of our group of travelers. From behind the tint in my sunglasses I could see men guarding luggage, women guarding children and Ethan leaning back against the wall. It didn't take long before the vibrations of the truck put me into a light but much needed sleep.

***

Covered in sweat, I awoke to the realization that half the passengers had migrated to the roof of the vehicle. To escape the heat, they were now sitting on the metal framework that made up the roof of the truck. Ethan was still sitting next to me only now he was engaged in a conversation with the African girl next to him. They noticed as I awoke and Ethan turned to include me in their conversation.

"Morning sunshine!" he said.

"Arrgh, why is it so hot?"

"Eh, it's not so bad. You're just weak! Guess what I found out?"

"What's that?"

"You see those three guys in the corner?"

"Yup. The ones that keep glancing over here?"

"Well, Gabra here tells me that they're planning on robbing us as soon as we leave our bags unattended."

"You're kidding!"

Ethan raised his eyebrows a bit in an attempt to show his seriousness.

"Okay, well we can work with that. Luckily there are two of us, so it shouldn't be a problem. One of us can always just stay with the bags."

"Alright, well I nominate you for first watch while we get food."

"What! We're getting food?" I said with excitement.

"Yeah, that's what Gabra said. Apparently we'll be stopping any time now. Ohh right, this is Gabra," he remembered that he should be polite and introduce us.

"Hello, nice to meet you!"

"Hello," she said back, with a big smile.

Gabra spoke very little and wore a traditional Muslim headdress that covered everything but her face. She presented herself with air of educated disdain as if she was exhausted from years of putting up with a culture that didn't suit her. Judging only from our brief encounter, I felt as if she carried a level of sophistication that easily surpassed the rest of us on the truck. It was as if she would be more suited for a town car than a freight truck.

Just as I was about to engage in a little light conversation with Gabra the truck began to slow down and pull off to the side of the road. We stopped at what appeared to be the Kenyan equivalent of a truck stop diner. The situation made me think of the random truck stop diners that my grandfather must have stopped at as he passed from town to town, driving semi trucks full of fruit. Although while his served steak and eggs ours would be serving up something slightly less familiar.

With me in charge of the bags, Ethan and Gabra jumped off the truck and made their way into the restaurant. As they walked away, I noticed out of the corner of my eye that Ethan way limping slightly.

"Hey! What's wrong with your leg?" I yelled.

"Actually it's my ankle," he replied. I scratched a mosquito bite or something and it started bleeding. I think it got infected, and now it hurts when I move it."

"Damn! You need to keep that clean then."

"Yeah, but that could be hard out here. I'll be fine, I just need to stop scratching it."

"Yeah you do! Have some self-control, you animal!"

All alone on the truck, I decided to get out and stretch my legs. I pulled our bags out from the truck and found a corner near the restaurant underneath some shade. Standing near my bag, I waited for Ethan to come back with two plates of something eatable. What I really wanted was a carne asada burrito, but that wasn't going to happen.

From outside I could see Ethan attempting to order our food. First looking confused as he glanced at everyone else's plates, then coming to a realization and looking sure of what he was going to order. The lady behind the counter prepared two plates for us, both exactly the same. Ethan made his way outside to where I was sitting and presented two plates of rice and beans with a side of fried banana.

I looked at the plates and shrugged, "Well, it's hard to complain about that. That's at least 70% of a burrito right there!"

"Watch out for rocks," Ethan said.

I looked at him confused, "What does that mean?"

"Rocks. Gabra said that a lot of time you find little pebbles in the beans. You don't want to chip a tooth out here so chew slow."

"Okay, good to know," I said as if I would have accepted any answer to that question.

We each sat there on our bags in the shade enjoying our food, just happy to be out of the truck. Gabra sat alone at a table in the far corner of the restaurant slowly eating a clump of ugali and sipping on an orange Fanta. From outside the restaurant we could see the three guys glancing our way as if hoping of catching us off guard. Unfortunately for them, we were well aware of their intentions. As we ate, no one said a word. Not us, not the people inside. All throughout the restaurant, the conversation was limited. We were all traveling together but we were strangers to each other.

After about 20 minutes everyone started to move and began climbing back on the truck. We promptly followed like the lost, out of place tourists that we were. For the duration of our journey we made sure to be careful with our bags, but we mostly remained casual as we talked to Gabra about her life in Northern Kenya.

It turned out that she was originally from Somalia. She had come to Kenya as a child with her parents who were fleeing from the chaos across the border. Up until the age of seven she lived in a refugee camp on the eastern side of the country where she spent most of her days helping her mother cook and clean. With no schools in the area, she learned to speak English from the NGO volunteers in her camp. These days she lived with her family on the outskirts of a small town called Maralal on the road south from Lake Turkana. She was heading back to the only place she could call home.

For the rest of the day, our journey carried on much the same as it had. And again, the terrain changed very little. The flat valley floor, that was becoming increasingly familiar, stretched on for miles in all directions. The landscape, dotted with bushes and acacia trees, still hot and sparsely populated with vegetation as well as with people, I felt as if we were alone in the middle of nowhere. At the same time I couldn't help but think that somewhere out there were people that wanted to either rob or kill us if they could. No matter. I decided to forget about that and read the final story in my father's envelope. There's no sense dwelling on things out of our control.

CHAPTER 17
A RELIGIOUS EXPERIENCE

On October 27, 1994 Mom convinced Dad to go into the local clinic for a full medical physical and checkup. The diagnosis was quick and it was clear; Dad had full stomach cancer and surgery was needed immediately.

All that summer Dad had been steadily losing weight. He had dropped from a solid muscular weight of near 230 pounds to a haggard appearing 170 pounds. He complained that his stomach was bothering him but we just thought it was the temporary flare-ups of an ulcer that had been diagnosed in the early spring of 1992. At that earlier time Dad had to be admitted to the hospital for stomach surgery but he came through it in relatively fine shape. It appeared, after that scare, that Dad would henceforth be fine so long as he stayed on the prescribed diet and medication.

But as the summer of 1994 wore on Dad began to lose weight. Nothing tasted good except vanilla milk shakes from the local Stamart Gas Station. Those he would consume at near four to five each day. When we would go out for lunch that summer Dad would usually order chicken and potatoes, but most often only picked at the potatoes and took most of the chicken home to his dogs. The more weight Dad lost that summer was that much more his dogs gained.

All during that summer of '94 Dad worked hard at his yard and his business ventures. For a six to eight week period surrounding the 4th of July the produce sales business was exceptionally busy. His trucks carrying fresh cherries, pears, peaches, cantaloupes, melons, and various other items were coming in nearly every day. Dad had to be there to receive and unload the produce, arrange and rearrange new and previously received produce, keep the displays in the store supplied and, with Mom and my sister Denise, run the business.

It was a given that during this time period his drivers would, depending on availability, be expected to help unload and arrange the incoming produce. Almost every time, without exception, that I was at the store during this time (which was usually four to five times each week) I would also be enlisted to help unload trucks and move pallets of produce. That summer all the drivers helped but none more so than Dad's nephew Bruce. Bruce would routinely drive all night to bring loads in and then stay for hours after coming in to help Dad unload the trailers and arrange the merchandise. On other days, days that were supposed to be Bruce's off days to rest before going out on a trip, Bruce would work from sun-up to sun-down with Dad. In all this time neither Bruce nor any of the other drivers would request any payment for this additional work.

Unquestionably, had it not been for the help of Bruce and the other drivers, Dad could possible have worked himself to an early death during that busy period.

In addition to the fruit business that summer, Dad continued his other business ventures. He had his trucking business, which required time each day to arrange loads (usually done with help from Mom), troubleshooting, loading and unloading schedules, overseeing repairs and breakdown problems, and all the other little things needed to keep the trucks on the road. Dad also was involved during this time period with his annual semi-trailer rentals to area fireworks dealers. He had made a number of commitments, as he did each year, to deliver storage trailers to the dealers for their firework season. Those trailers had to be delivered, set in place, and then later at the end of the season, retrieved and (on some occasions) cleaned of debris.

Additionally Dad was continuing his business/hobby of buying and selling used cars. Every other Saturday that summer Dad would go to a local used car auction, conveniently located just down the highway from him, and bid and bargain for any number and types of used cars. Occasionally he would sell a car or two but usually he preferred to buy only, and sell to various individuals who would stop in the yard on a near continuous basis. I was his bookkeeper for this venture and in the summer of 1994 alone Dad completed transactions on over 30 vehicles, sometimes buying and selling and re-buying the same vehicle, often taking trade-ins and occasionally offering and providing financing to prospective buyers.

And in addition to all of those things that Dad was juggling that summer he also decided to undertake two other major endeavors. Dad wanted to build a new unloading dock (which he did, a near 1,000 square foot concrete dock with ramp) and he wanted to do some yard cleaning (which he also did, near 400 tons of iron and steel, and truck cabs, wheels and parts). That summer, during a six-week period before his hospital experience, Dad was able to clear out a near 20-year accumulation of truck parts and pieces. He finally decided he no longer needed a rear-end for a '42 Chevy Truck or a driveshaft for a '66 Mack. No other single person could possibly have accomplished such a major cleaning in such a short time. All of us in the family were amazed to learn there was a cornfield behind our yard; how did that get there?

With all of the above going on, and with Dad not eating properly, we all were not surprised that Dad was losing weight. We attributed the weight loss to hard work and improper diet due to lack of appetite. We attributed the lack of appetite to his sensitive stomach. All during this weight loss Mom kept pushing Dad to get a more thorough checkup; she knew intuitively that there was more wrong with Dad then an ulcer that had supposedly been cured.

When that full physical was finally accomplished, that day in late October 1994, then we finally knew, we thought, the extent of the problem. Surgery for removal of his stomach was scheduled for the next week and Dad was admitted to the hospital on Thursday, November 3rd. Mom and I took Dad in for admittance at 6AM on that scheduled day. My sister Denise joined us shortly after that time as Dad was being prepared.

Surgery was expected to be serious but successful. The doctors anticipated, based on the tests taken the week before that a portion of Dad's stomach would be removed. We were informed that an operation of this nature was not unusual and was considered relatively low risk.

At mid-morning the surgeon informed us that the cancer was more widespread than first believed. The entire stomach would have to be removed, as well as the spleen and possibly the pancreas. It was hoped that no other organs would be involved.

The time during the initial operation was difficult for the family. Denise and I were in near constant phone contact with our other siblings Alex, Brian, and Randy on an almost hourly basis during that period of time. We were also in contact with other family members and close family friends. The consensus we had, even after it was known that the surgery would be more extensive then first believed, was that no one of the out of state family would plan to fly back; we all believed Dad would recover from the surgery without any problem and then we could all congregate at Thanksgiving, which was only two weeks away.

And after the surgery was completed it appeared that our instincts of Dad's full recovery would be correct. Dad was quickly moved from Intensive Care (after only one day there) to a regular hospital room. The doctor labeled the surgery as successful but he warned us that during the recovery there were two important things to guard against; blood clots and infection.

During this recovery period Dad was hooked up to various tubes and support devices. As each day went by the tubes and devices began to disappear. On the third day of recovery Dad was up walking the halls, supported by a walker and a nurse on either side and with his connecting tubes and tube tree following. The nurses were continually telling him "Homer, slow down…Homer, slow down". During all of this the doctors continued to monitor and test his progress and it appeared a full and successful recovery could be expected.

While Dad was making this recovery, we were becoming slowly dissatisfied with the nursing care being given to Dad. Several of the nurses were exceptionally good and contentious, but others appeared a little lax and as if the entire process was a bother to them.

Mom was especially unhappy with the care Dad was receiving. On several occasions Mom had to remind the attending nurse to reconnect a leg-massaging unit after coming back from a walk. On various other occasions we all noted that the nurses and the aids could not reset the various alarm bottoms, which occasionally rang when feeding or medicine bags became low. On one occasion, only three or four days into the recovery while Dad was still being fed by a tube, a nurse brought a full meal into the room. By this time Dad also had lost confidence in the nurse's abilities. When he saw the food he only mumbled to her "Room 237"? By saying "Room 237" to her, the nurse then realized she was delivering the food to the wrong room.

And yet another time a nurse came into the room and started moving Dad around to put him on a transporting bed. Dad assumed he was being prepared for another test or some other routine review but he did decide to ask what was being planned.

"Oh" the nurse said, looking at her clipboard, "we're going to prep you now for your heart surgery."

Dad: "Heart surgery?"

Nurse: "Yes, your heart surgery."

Dad: "Room 237."

Nurse: "Oh…Never mind."

It could have been worse; it could have been for a sex change operation.

With this type of care we decided to stay with Dad nearly all the time, including all day and night time hours. We couldn't read the machines or administer the medicine, but we knew Dad couldn't have solid food and we knew he wasn't scheduled for any heart surgery.

Between Mom, Denise, my wife Kim, Bruce and I, we were able to stay with Dad nearly every minute. Dad constantly wanted ice for his dry mouth and we were able to keep him supplied when his nurses became too busy with other patients to bring it to him.

During this recovery time we continued to call out to family members and friends with updates, especially to our brother Randy who was becoming increasingly perturbed with reports of nurse error and indifference. Randy threatened to write a letter to the hospital (which is a lawyer's way of punching someone in the nose) but Dad heard of his intent on this and asked he not do it. Dad liked both of his doctors and several of the nurses and he didn't care to make any big deal of any of the issues.

As Dad was recovering, his sense of humor began to return. At one point, when a business associate was wishing him well and assuring him that he would soon be sending Dad a payment for some truck part recently purchased, Dad only grunted and said well, if you don't, we'll have to have Randy send you a letter. At another time while visiting yet another business associate and friend, a nurse came into the room to tell Dad that in a few minutes they would be taking him for some x-rays. The friend asked Dad why x-rays were needed, wasn't the surgery successful? Dad just opened one eye and said "The doc thinks he lost a glove".

Up to this point, regardless of our concerns with a few of the nurses assigned to Dad, the recovery appeared to be going fine. But Mom was suspicious; she had a premonition that Dad was not quite as healthy and strong as he appeared. Because of Mom's concern, either Bruce, her or I stayed every night to watch Dad. Denise and Kim came in during the early morning hours and during the day to allow us to get some sleep and time away from the hospital.

As it turned out Mom's instincts were right about having to stay with Dad during the recovery, especially at night. In the early hours of Monday, November 14, Dad was helped out of his bed by his nurse in preparation for an early morning walk. The nurse had to leave the room for a minute and she left Dad standing, supporting himself against a wheel chair. Immediately after she left the room Dad began to turn a pale color and began gasping for breath. Mom caught Dad to keep him from falling and recalled the nurse for help.

At that point things began to happen fast.

The in-house doctor on duty was immediately called and Dad was stabilized. This action caused Dad to lose all consciousness. Additional tubes and wires and other monitoring devices were installed on Dad and he was transported back to an Intensive Care room. During this process Mom called both Denise and I and we were back at the hospital in a very short period of time. By midmorning we were informed that Dad had developed serious blood clotting in his lungs. It appeared the clots had been in his legs, and when he stood up that morning, those clots traveled up and through his heart and into the lungs. He also had a very serious infection at or near the point of the cancer surgery.

The doctors informed us that kidney failure and/or

heart failure and/or lung failure and/or brain damage were all possible. Immediate measures were being taken to restore oxygen into the lungs and further measures would have to be taken that day, pending ongoing testing, to combat and defend against these possible adverse events.

Survival rate, assuming no heart-lung-brain-kidney or other major organ damage, was calculated at 40%.

During this time of testing Dad was completely unconscious. A breathing mask was strapped to his mouth and nose to provide pure oxygen. In the previous week Dad had used that same mask in 30 minute increments only two or three times each day. It was simply too exhausting to use for any greater period of time; now Dad would have his mask on him for the next 30 hours. Each breath was an absolute supreme effort by Dad. Every time he breathed in his chest would rise four or more inches; when the breath was expelled he would sink back down and into the bed. Dad took each breath like a man who had just sprinted a mile. During all this time, the entire 30 hours, he was completely drenched in sweat and his skin over his entire body was icy cold to the touch.

Despite the obvious pain and effort Dad had to make to take each breath the doctors insisted there was, at that time, no other choice. If his heart were to start failing, they said, they would put him on a respirator. But using a respirator would further decrease his chance for survival by another 13%.

On Wednesday morning, after Dad had struggled for those long hours with the mask the doctors decided they had no choice but to remove the mask and install a respirator. It became too clear that Dad could not continue to maintain the strength that was needed to breathe. He had struggled for nearly 30 continuous hours and now the strength of his heart was of concern. We knew that the use of the respirator decreased his survival rate but without it we couldn't see how he could survive much longer without heart failure.

By Thursday of that week, after numerous and continuous tests had been performed, the doctors determined that additional surgery would be necessary. By this time Dad was breathing easier, with the help of the respirator, and it appeared as if the blood clots in the lungs were being successfully dissipated. But there was still an area in his lower chest area that was severely infected, and that area had to be cleaned and treated, and those remaining organs (primarily the kidneys, the lungs, and the liver) had to be checked for infection.

To do this surgery it was necessary to take some precaution to prevent additional blood clots from moving from the legs up into the lungs. The doctors decided to install small filters on the main veins of the legs, thereby trapping any further clots that might be migrating upward. We were told that filters, in and by itself, were not usually considered major surgery. In this case however, with Dad still in an unconscious condition, still having some lingering effects of the previous blood clots in the lungs, and still not recovered from the surgery for the cancer (which was performed only the previous week) the doctors considered this as a major event.

That Thursday morning the filters of the legs were installed and appeared to be successful. The next step, within the next few hours would be to now reopen the area of the cancer surgery and attempt to find a reason and cause for the massive infection Dad was experiencing. Again the concerns of prior yet unhealed surgery were present as well as the greatly weakened condition of Dad for all the other problems. Within an hour or so of the filter surgery Dad was once again on the operating table for the exploratory surgery.

At this point Dad had been unconscious or semi-conscious for nearly 80 hours. The doctors now were not telling us of any estimate of his survival rate. Whereas it had previously been 40%, then 27%, then less then 10%, now they were only saying that Dad, even if he survived the next surgery, may be facing potential major problems with his heart, lungs, kidneys and brain. The doctors advised us to meet with our family minister.

The exploratory surgery began and finished in the late afternoon of that Thursday. The results were surprising. Dad had absolutely no infection in the area of the cancer surgery. The infection was coming from a totally unrelated source; Dad had a badly inflamed appendix. It was a surprise to the doctors. Although the doctors would not comment on the success of this third surgery, we thought it was the best possible news we could have received. No infection was present, as far as could be determined, on any of the major organs of the area and no damage could be detected in the spine or the brain.

By finding an inflamed appendix the puzzle was answered (what was causing the infection?) and the solution was obvious and routine (remove the appendix).

After that surgery the doctors informed us that they had done nearly everything to Dad that could be done. His stomach, spleen, and part of his pancreas had been removed by the first surgery; filters to avoid blood clots had been installed in his legs in the second surgery; and his appendix had been removed in the third surgery. Additionally tests for damage to the lungs, spine, kidneys, and brain, had been, and were continuing to be run. Now it would be up to Dad to awake from those surgeries and to heal.

During all this time the family had come home to give Mom support and to encourage Dad to recover. From as far as California, Idaho and snow covered rural North Dakota, people came. All the incoming family members had, I think; with a firm belief that all would be fine. We all knew Dad; if a doctor said one man in 100 could survive any given ordeal, we knew that Dad would be that one man. We had all seen Dad, time after time again, encounter and defy those and slimmer odds in his business dealings and method of business management.

But as each family member arrived and was able to view Dad, and was able to see first hand how desperately Dad was trying to hang on, with tubes and needles and nurses and doctors all around him, it became clearer that their trip home was maybe not to cheer Dad on, but maybe to say goodbye. We could only hope that Dad could hear us in his coma, or at least that his spirit was in the room and could see us around his bed.

Some of us had an advantage over the other family members over the extent that we had seen Dad in his bad and deteriorating condition for several days. We had the time to reconcile ourselves for the worst. By the time of the critical operation of that Thursday, when other family members were still in a belief that Dad might recover, we were instead thinking about life after Dad; how to continue his business affairs, how to adjust without him, and how Mom would be able to cope living out at the house by herself.

Throughout this difficult time we were all visited by numerous family friends who provided a great comfort, both to us, Dad and especially to Mom.

All day Thursday, into the night, we all as a family stayed at the hospital to await Dad's awakening from his coma. We were confident, even if his doctors weren't that the recent surgeries and testing would be successful. We slept in shifts at the hospital with two or three of us at a time at Dad's bedside. We were relentless in trying to get Dad to respond to us; we massaged his arms and legs, talked and joked with him (and about him), tickled his feet, and did anything else we could think of to coax or irritate him into opening his eyes.

At midmorning on that Friday, Kim was in the recovery room with Dad and the rest of us were several rooms away in a waiting room. Half of us were sleeping or nearly sleeping. All of a sudden we hear a person racing down the hall toward us, rounding the corner, and flying into the room. It's Kim (fleet-footed Kim we now call her) telling us that "Homer's opened his eyes, Homer's opened his eyes!!" Other people in the waiting room (perhaps on the entire floor) may not have known who Homer was but they knew he had opened his eyes.

Kim gets excited when she finds a dime on the sidewalk, so this really had her worked up.

We all immediately erupted from the waiting room all except me; I was in the bathroom. My brother-in-law Tim had the presence of mind to come back and get me. Sure enough, with some coaxing and prodding, Dad would try to raise his eyebrow and would try to give Mom's hand a squeeze. He was responding.

That event marked a turning point. From then on, over the next few days and also into the weekend, Dad began to respond with slight movements of his feet and hands. The doctors were amazed. One doctor termed Dad a "superman" for what he had been through; a second doctor called the entire event a miracle; and a third noted that the recovery that he had witnessed from Dad was a textbook case.

That doctor only had to ask us prior to any of these events. We knew for years that Dad had made it a regular course of his life to defy odds; we also knew for years that our Dad was a textbook case.

Dad continued to improve slowly and was eventually released to a thankful family in December. In all, Dad had undergone three separate and major surgeries, had left the hospital with four less organs than when he first arrived (leaving behind a stomach, spleen, pancreas, and appendix) and had, during the worst of the times, 16 or so separate tubes and wires and probes attached and connected into him.

We feel it was the support of the family and friends, even as much as the skill of the surgeons and nurses that pulled Dad through. Absolutely, without any doubt, it could not have been accomplished without God's intervention.

Interestingly enough, during the later days of this ordeal, Paul Harvey News reported that the San Francisco General Hospital had just conducted a study that showed a definite and significant link between prayer and recovery with critically ill patients. They didn't tell any of us anything we didn't know.

CHAPTER 18
MARSABIT

DAY ONE:

By the time we arrived in Marsabit it was dark and the town was quiet. I couldn't make any real assessment on what type of place it was but at that moment I didn't truly care. There was very little light on the streets and no signs of life, so we followed the largest group of people toward a two story yellow structure around the corner from where we were dropped off. It was a hotel, and probably the only one in town.

The entrance consisted of flimsy metal door propped open with a bungee cord and a brick. A single light bulb hung from its wire and flickered near the front entrance. The word "hotel" was hand-painted on the side of the wall in simple black lettering. Without much consideration, we followed the group into the lobby and queued up to reserve a room. The man at the front desk looked tired and unimpressed by the recent influx of people. He quickly got through the line of people by exchanging a few words, accepting a payment and handing them their key. Our transaction was no different.

"Hello, " I said.

"Hello, for two?" he replied.

"Yes,"

"Room 16, second floor. In the morning, there is a free breakfast in the kitchen."

"Okay, great."

"Breakfast is over at 9AM. That will be 600 Shillings," he concluded.

Behind the counter, in the corner I could see a small six-inch television set that was on but muted slightly. It seemed as if our group of travelers had interrupted his program, which explained the promptness of our service. In an attempt to limit our impact on this man's evening, we paid and took our key without asking any additional questions.

The hotel was a large establishment that appeared to be nearly empty. The rooms wrapped around the outer wall of the building with an open courtyard in the middle. From the second floor landing we could look down onto the first floor below. In the center of the courtyard was what appeared to be an indoor pond, now dried up and rusting. Surrounding the pond was a display of fake plants and shrubbery like the kind you might find in a dentist's office. The kitchen was on the second floor adjacent to our room with the communal restrooms were down the hallway.

The hotel could have looked far worse; it wouldn't have mattered. Any bed was better than a bag of rock hard beans to sleep on. Marsabit was another sleepy town and as a result we went to bed almost immediately that night.

***

I awoke the next day to Ethan barging back into the room after his morning shower.

"Dude!" he exclaimed. "We should go to Lake Turkana!"

"We should, why?"

"Because, it looks sweet…and because they found tons of hominid remains there!

"Oh yeah?" I said, still groggy.

"Yeah, you know, hominids…humans before they

148

were really human like us."

"Okay, but since when do you care about archeology?"

"Since this morning when I read about it in this book," he said with a smirk.

"Okay well, how do we get there then?"

He thought for a while, "I'm not sure. We'll figure it out. Hey, get your ass up! I'm starving."

At his request I managed to drag myself out of bed, shower up and get dressed in record time. I met Ethan at the second floor kitchen for our free breakfast. It consisted of an omelet, baked beans, two pieces of toast and a half cut tomato. A pretty solid score considering it was free. Then came the coffee, another cup of NesCafé instant coffee. It started to feel like I wouldn't be able to get a good cup of Kenyan coffee until I got back home and ordered one from Starbucks.

After breakfast we reconvened outside the hotel underneath the shade of a freight truck. We were rested, fed and ready for something, but what? With no plan and virtually no information available on this town we simply began to wander straight down the main road and explore. Although there wasn't much to it; a few food stalls and some corner stores, a herd of goats here and there, and people just moving about their day. Shooting off of the main road were the winding side streets where most of the people lived. A quick survey revealed that most of the homes in this town were small huts surrounded by areas of farmland.

From where we stood near the side of a corner store, it felt like we could see the edge of town. In front we could see only a few scattered homes that remained and then the town just seemed to stop, with only the never-ending expanse of savanna behind it.

From out of nowhere a young kid approached us with a big smile on his face. He was probably about 17 years old, but I couldn't be sure. He wore a backwards blue baseball cap that had the letters "LA" embroidered on the front and baggy blue jeans with a grey t-shirt. Obviously heavily influenced by American hip-hop culture, he was eager to meet some outsiders. Hip-hop has penetrated nearly every corner of the world, at the moment its one of our most influential cultural exports.

"Hello!" he said with excitement. "How are you?"

He seemed to be happy to practice his English.

"Good!" I replied. "How are you?"

"Welcome to Marsabit! My name is Terry. Why do you come to our village?" He said again with a big smile instead of responding to my question.

As we spoke, I noticed that he had an entourage of friends standing behind him. They all watched in amazement as he made contact with us. Perhaps he was the only one who could speak English or perhaps he was just the only one outgoing enough to speak to total strangers. Regardless, it appeared that we had made a friend.

"We are just exploring your town and we'd also like to visit Lake Turkana. Is that possible?" I asked hoping to get some information right away.

"Yes, of course!" he replied. "You can take a truck to Lake Turkana! It's very nice. Many trucks will ride together, but sometimes they do not come. You will need to wait and see."

"Is there a way to find out when the next truck to Lake Turkana will come?"

"No, not possible. You can wait here and if one comes, then you can go," he pointed to the grassy knoll next to us.

It did in fact look like the most logical place to wait for a ride. I'll have to give him that.

"Okay, do you think they will come today?"

"Yes, maybe later," Terry replied.

We both weren't too thrilled with his casual responses but I had expected things to work this way. We were pretty far removed from the luxuries of timetables and schedules.

"Okay, thank you so much!" Ethan said. "Maybe we'll

wait for the truck there then."

"Yes, please," he said, as he gestured to the grassy knoll.

With nothing left to explore, we went back to the hotel, grabbed our bags and set up shop at the grassy knoll in hopes that a convoy would pass through. We each purchased two "mango drinks" to help pass the time underneath the hot sun. They came in tiny juice boxes and lasted a total of 15 seconds each, but well worth it as they are packed with sugar and mango-y goodness.

A few hours passed that mostly included smoking, listening to music and trying to chat with the local tribes women, who were also there waiting for something. They however didn't speak any English so this made things difficult. I could tell by the way they were dressed that they were from the Turkana tribe, a very famous tribe in Kenya due to the fact that they are one of the few tribes left that refuse to change their traditional customs. So to this day, they still dress in traditional Turkana cloths, which usually includes a red dress, tons of jewelry, piercings and a dagger or a spear.

As the hours passed, the day began to wind down and we started to think about cutting our losses and trying to find a local bar, when Terry showed up once again.

"Hello my friends! How are you?"

"Good," I said. "But there are still no trucks to Lake Turkana."

"No, no. Not today." he said, as he looked around. "But you can come see my village!" He burst out with excitement.

We both looked at each other and decided that it was a pretty good plan, given the circumstances. We went back to our hotel, dropped off our bags and met Terry outside for the grand tour of Marsabit.

As we walked around the village, it was clear that everyone here knew everyone else. They all seemed thrilled that he had "found" a couple of foreigners to take around.

We walked through sections where women tended to gardens, children played with hand-made toys and mothers pounded corn into ugali. We saw smiles on the faces of people who lived in huts with dirt floors, yet right next to their closest friends and family.

Ethan was still limping and by this time was having a real hard time walking. I was getting worried that he needed to see a doctor. He was limping more with each step and it was becoming very noticeable.

"Are you okay?" asked Terry

"Yeah, I'm fine," Ethan said softly. "I just have a bad mosquito bite."

Terry looked closer, "Oh no! You need medicine. This is very bad!"

I gave Ethan a distressed look.

Ethan brushed it off, "Guys, don't worry. I'll be fine."

Ethan hated it when people would worry about him. So with that in mind we let it go, but I still felt that we needed to keep an eye on it. The last thing we wanted was a medical emergency out in the middle of nowhere. Terry looked concerned as well.

After a significant period of time was spent walking around the village Terry said he needed to stop off and quickly see a friend who was sick.

"I only need to say hello for five minutes. Okay?"

"Yeah, of course," Ethan replied.

"Okay, I will be right back."

There in the street we stood, waiting as he visited his sick friend. Looking at Ethan, I could tell that he was in pain.

"I really don't like the look of that foot. We should try to find a doctor tomorrow before we leave town."

"What? For a mosquito bite! That seems a little excessive. I just need to keep it clean and the infection will heal in no time," he said with confidence.

"Well, why haven't you been able to do that so far?"

"'Cause, it's crazy dirty and sweaty out here!" he said

defensively.

"So what makes you think you can do that tomorrow and the next day?"

"Just don't worry about me. I'll let you know if I need a doctor!" he said in an attempt to end the conversation.

Just then, sure enough, Terry was back.

"Hey, is everything okay?" I asked.

"Yes, yes. He will be fine. He is sick with malaria and has a bad fever so he must stay in bed," he replied casually.

"What?" Ethan exclaimed. "Malaria! Isn't that deadly?"

"Yes it can be, but it is not so bad when you are older. When you are small like a baby, that is the worst," Terry explained.

"I don't know, I just remember hearing about people always dying from malaria."

"Yes, yes. Sometimes, but mostly young children and babies. For example, I get malaria at least one time every year, and I am fine."

"One time per year?" Ethan shouted with his mouth hanging open. "You must have a pretty strong immune system."

"Haha, yes maybe so," Terry replied with a smile as he began to lead us back to the town center.

After a full day of walking, the day was nearing an end and we were exhausted. We had seen the homes back in the dirt roads that surrounded the main street. We had visited Terry's sick friend and seen all the "notable places" of this little African town. As our tour of Marsabit was winding down, we decided to finish our day at the local town bar with a couple of Tuskers and some rice and beans. The bar was nothing special, just another non-descript cement storefront with red plastic chairs. But it had beer, food and a great view of the main road, and therefore it was a great place to end the day. Terry was no doubt at home, spending the evening with his family.

***

DAY TWO:

We woke early and made our way to the grassy waiting knoll, sitting once again on top of our bags with the same Turkana tribe's women as the day before. It appeared that we were all waiting on the same convoy. It was like being at an office job. The day just dragged on yet nothing really happened. Cigarettes and mango juice, rice and beans. There was nothing to do in this tiny town after seeing everything the prior day.

At this point, Ethan's foot was looking really bad. He limped with each step and even had a hard time wearing flip-flops as the swelling in his foot made it painful and difficult to put them on. By now there was no possible way he could even put a shoe on his foot. The color had changed from a light red to a shiny purple and the infected bite itself was starting to turn blackish.

"Dude, your foot looks like shit!" I said calmly but seriously.

"Yeah, I know. I think I need to get this looked at."

It wasn't like Ethan to admit needing a doctor so I knew we were in a bad situation.

"I agree. Okay, you wait here for a truck and I'll go walk around town and see if I can find a doctor or somewhere that sells medicine."

"Get me some narcotics too!" he said jokingly. "You know...for the pain."

I looked back smiling, "Let's try to stay focused here."

I made my way back into the village away from the main road where we had been waiting. If there were a doctor's office or pharmacy on the main road, we would have seen it by now. From the very beginning the search didn't look promising. You always hear stories of isolated African villages without access to healthcare, and this was starting to look like a prime example.

I searched through nearly every street and alleyway.

Every so often I would try to ask someone where I could find a doctor or a pharmacy, and every answer I received was either a "No" or a confused look. After an hour of searching, the verdict was clear. We needed to get out of Marsabit immediately. I knew our best bet to find what we needed was in the town of Isiolo, south of Marsabit by about six hours. But this was a very difficult stretch of road, one that was under constant threat of bandits and tribal warfare. If a convoy wasn't available we would need to find another way south, and this meant taking on a big risk.

Back at the grassy knoll I explained to Ethan what the situation was. He didn't seem shocked in the slightest. Even a quick glance at this place and you could probably guess that there was a serious lack of healthcare available.

"So I guess Lake Turkana is out of the question then?" he said, knowing the answer.

"I'd say so. I can't imagine there will be any doctors there either, and it's in the opposite direction of Isiolo. If we don't get you something for your foot, I'm afraid it could get really bad. You could even lose it."

With those words, it was as if a wave of reality hit him in the face. He knew as well as I did that infections can spread quickly when unattended and his was looking pretty grim at this point.

The sun was setting and another day became a total bust. We made our way back to the local bar, our new favorite hangout spot, for what was hopefully our last Tusker in Marsabit. In the morning we desperately needed to leave this town, now for reasons outside our growing boredom.

***

DAY THREE:

We awoke earlier than usual in hopes of catching the

first moving vehicle south to Isiolo. In a serious attempt to leave town we sat in the grassy knoll with our bags packed and two cups of instant coffee, a pineapple and a bundle of bananas for breakfast. At this point we were prepared to forgo our safety for some healthcare...or at least some medicine.

Ethan's foot was only getting worse. He was unable to walk without leaning on my shoulder for support. Every time he put pressure on his foot, he could barely stand it. The purple color had increased around the wound and the red color that surrounded it had spread even further. The center, where the initial bite was, was now a dark black. I knew from what my mother had told me about infections as a child that if you ever were to see a red streak spreading out from a wound, you had a blood infection. And that was what I was most worried about now.

As we sat there once again eating our breakfast with the tribal women, Terry showed up as if he knew we would still be there. In towns of this size everyone is aware of when a convoy rolls through town. It's actually a kind of a big deal.

"My friends! How is your time in Marsabit? I see you do not wish to leave us!" he said in a cheery sarcastic tone.

"Good, good," I said, trying to exchange formalities quickly. "But we still haven't seen any trucks."

"But I think today the trucks will come!" he tried to assure us.

"What makes you say that?"

"It has been three days since the last group, maybe it's a good day for another."

This was not the kind of logic I was looking for.

Ethan interjected, "Terry, is there another way to get to Nairobi?"

"I thought you wanted to visit Lake Turkana?" Terry replied, surprised.

"No, my foot is fucked up and I need to get to a doctor."

Terry looked at his foot, "Oh my god! Yes, your foot is fucked up! You should go to Nairobi...not to Lake Turkana. Maybe you can go to Isiolo...it is much closer."

"That's what we were thinking," I said.

"Yes, but you need to travel in convoy if you go south. It is not safe to go alone."

"Well, we may have to take that risk. His foot is starting to become a serious health concern. Are there any single trucks or cars going that way today?"

He thought for a moment, "Maybe there is one going, but it is dangerous."

It was 10AM when our conversation had finished and about 11AM when he came rushing back, "Hello! Hello! I have found a ride for you!"

We both jumped up off our bags, "You did! That's great! Is it going to Nairobi or Isiolo?"

"Yes, it is going to Isiolo today, but it will leave very soon...maybe in 20 minutes."

"Perfect! How much is it?"

"It will cost you 700 shillings each," he said.

"Okay, that sounds great...thanks so much!"

As we started to get our things together in order to leave at a moments notice, he stopped us suddenly.

"But my friends, you must not stop on the road," he said in the most serious tone I had heard him use up to now. "This is a very dangerous road and if you stop, you will not be safe. Eleven people have been killed since you arrived. The tribes are fighting now."

This was news to us.

"Okay, but what if the driver stops?"

"He will not want to. Also, keep your heads down when you pass by others. Do not let them see your face. Muzungus are bigger targets."

His words conveyed the seriousness of our situation and his once carefree persona had been replaced by a firm warning of danger. It was strange to think of Kenya as being a hotspot for bandits and killings. After all, this was the home of the great east African safaris, tourism and Swahili culture. But that's all in the south. This is the north and despite being within the same borders, they are worlds apart. At this point it didn't matter much. Whatever the risks, we needed to get to Isiolo…and soon.

From out of nowhere a dirty white pickup truck pulled up around the corner near the grassy knoll. As it stopped suddenly near us it created a dust cloud that filled the air around us. Terry walked up to the man driving the vehicle and spoke to him in a dialect I couldn't recognize. There were two men in front and two in the back. The back of the pickup truck had no seating other than an old tire, a wooden crate and a couple mounds produced by the piling up of a few scattered tools and chains.

"Okay, you can pay the man for two people. He will take you to Isiolo. From there you can go to Nairobi. You can sit in the back."

We did as Terry suggested and took our places at the rear of the truck. Ethan and I did our best to make seats out of the mounds of tools and chains and wrapped bandanas around our heads to block the scorching sun as we began to settle in for the long journey south.

Ethan reached out his hand, "Terry, thank you so much for everything! You've got a great village here."

"Oh thank you. It was nice to meet you. Can I take your emails?"

"Of course!"

Ethan pulled out a piece of scrape paper and wrote down our email addresses for Terry, although I didn't expect to be hearing from him any time soon. I doubted if he got the chance to get online very often. It was more of a nice gesture, as we knew we were unlikely to see each other ever again.

As we pulled away from the grassy knoll in another cloud of dust, we waved goodbye to Terry and the tribal women who were still waiting for the convoy to come and take them further down the road. We had spent only three days in Marsabit but somehow it felt like we were leaving something more profound. I guess you can really get to know a place when you spend three days on a grassy knoll watching life go by.

CHAPTER 19
THE PICKUP TRUCK

It didn't take long to get out of town, a few minutes at most and despite the potential for danger, I felt good about our decision to leave. For the first time in days I felt like we were finally making some progress.

We were unable to communicate with any of the people in the truck, and this included the driver. Although it didn't matter much, the wind and the rumbling of the vehicle produced more noise than we could have shouted over. But despite our lack of communication, the smiles on our fellow travelers faces were comforting enough to let us know that we were okay, at least for the moment.

Like everyday, the sun was hot but this time we had the breeze of the passing air by to cool us down. This was however deceiving, as we would still burn badly if we didn't cover our entire bodies. We both sat in the back of the dusty pickup truck wearing long pants, bandanas and scarves in the scorching heat, hiding everything but our eyes from the sun and any potential onlookers.

The scenery was much like before with vast expanses of grassland dotted with occasional acacia trees. The road was bumpy and full of potholes that made it hard to move quickly, but in Kenya they've learned how to work around it. The northern part of the country was long neglected by the Kenyan government as they claimed that its residents were "savages" and un-governable". I will respectfully disagree, but as a result, the infrastructure is in desperate need of repair.

We had traveled about 20 minutes outside of Marsabit when out of nowhere we felt a large *bang* from the front of the truck. It felt as if we hit a wall but somehow kept moving we forward. From the back of the truck we could hear the sound of our right front tire slowly deflating as we began to pull off on the side of the road.

Despite all of Terry's warnings, we were now stopped on the side of the road in north Kenyan, bandit country.

We didn't need language to understand what everyone was feeling on that truck. We all got off and went around front to the damaged tire. They spoke in their local dialect as we all stood there looking at the damage, just like all men do in all countries when something mechanical needs to be done. Although within seconds, the driver and front passenger began to fix the flat tire. It was as if they didn't want to be there any longer than we had to. And now the spare tire and tools in the back of the truck made a lot more sense. I just hoped we wouldn't need another.

I surveyed the landscape as they jacked up the truck and replaced the tire. I had the strange expectation of seeing camouflaged men with guns rolling up in armed vehicles. But that never happened. Within minutes the tire was fixed, we were reassembled in our respective seats and we were back on the road. Uneventful, and that's how we liked it.

As we made our way south to Isiolo, we could see our surroundings changing. Villages became more frequent and populations became denser. As we peered out from underneath our bandanas and sunglasses we could see for the first time, the beginning of a new landscape. Herders with goats, grazing in the distance, primates rustling in the trees and the occasional herd of wild giraffe feeding on the leaves of the tallest trees. At one point, the giraffe became so common that they managed to block traffic as they slowly crossed the road in front of us.

We were beginning to leave the "Wild West" of Kenya

and approach civilization once again. As we moved further south, a sense of relief washed over me as the realization that our decision to leave Marsabit was turning out to be a good one. Soon we would be in Isiolo, and Ethan would be able to find a doctor.

CHAPTER 20
ISIOLO

We arrived in Isiolo after dark, and I was afraid that even if this town had doctors or pharmacies they would all be closed by now. Ethan's foot was only getting worse.

As the truck slowed down and pulled over on the side of the main road, it was as if we had stepped into another world. They say that Isiolo is a frontier town on the border of the "Wild West", and it felt like exactly that. The streets were crowded with people just hanging out, yelling, drinking, smoking and driving insanely. Motorcycles raced loudly up and down the streets in the night, like from a scene out of a post-apocalyptic movie. Our driver had dropped us off right in the middle of all the madness and from there we walked...and limped, in search of a place to stay for the night.

Luckily in a town this lively it would be easy to find a place to sleep. Rule of thumb, just look for the glowing neon sign that says "Hotel". The place we ended up finding, was a big building with an open courtyard in the middle and a locking gate. The rooms were basic and cheap. Below us was a bar where hookers hung out offering their services to transient men while they passed the time by drinking themselves into a stupor. We would not be joining their party.

Ethan was nearly unable to walk at this point so while he laid on the bed in the hotel room, I went out in search of drugs. At this point any antibiotics would do, regardless of their intended use.

"Alright, I'll be back as soon as I can find something."

"Sounds good, I'll just be here. Oh, and even if you can't find any antibiotics still bring back some beers."

"Sure, I'll see what I can do."

Most of the reputable establishments in town were closed and what remained mostly consisted of bars, nightclubs and shops. My hope was to find something that looked official enough to sell real, and safe, antibiotics. I wasn't very hopeful.

As I walked the streets, I asked around to the best of my ability and people kept pointing me in the same direction. So it only made sense to follow that direction which happened to be down the main road about five blocks or so. As the lights and noise of central Isiolo began to fade away, I could see another neon light off in the distance. As it came into focus my excitement grew, and I began to make out the words "Drug Store".

With an increased pace I started to walk faster toward the storefront, and as the lights got clearer, I became more hopeful. When all of a sudden I could see that, to my disappointment, only the neon sign remained turned on, casting light all around the store windows and the sidewalk below. The store was empty, dark inside and closed.

I walked back feeling defeated and wondering if Ethan would be okay for another day without drugs or a doctor. I wasn't sure, but had to believe that he would be.

After an additional search of the town over the next hour and a half, I found myself exhausted and sitting at an outdoor bar just around the corner from our hotel. Just one beer to end the night, I thought. Ethan would surely be asleep by now and I was in no mood to rest. Staring at the night sky and the chaos around me from the patio chairs, I was almost instantly approached by a friendly voice from inside the bar.

"Hello mate!" he said.

From the darkness he slowly came into focus as he

approached. I could tell by his accent that he was a Welshman, and the first other foreigner I'd seen in days.

"I didn't expect to see another muzungu in these parts! How ya doin?"

"I'm good," I said, surprised as well to see another foreigner in Isiolo.

"Mind if I join ya?"

"No, of course not! Have a seat."

I had to admit, it was nice to see another foreign face. Even though I wasn't in much of a celebratory mood, it had been a long time. And he was as close as anything there was to familiar around northern Kenya.

Over the course of a few beers, we exchanged the typical words that travelers tend to when they meet one another. Where are you from? Where have you been? Where are you going?....that sort of thing.

His name was Gareth and he was working as an English teacher in Uganda. He said that he had hoped to take a trip up to Lake Turkana but had decided against it at the last minute.

"Wow! So you came from up north? That's amazing! I've been told that it's not safe to make the trip," he said as if he was half jealous and half impressed.

"Well, we didn't have much choice. Once you get so far, it only makes sense to keep going rather than head back all the way to where you started. We would have probably done some things differently but my brother fucked up his foot and needs to see a doctor. By the way, do you know if there's a doctor in town here?"

"Oh too bad. No, I don't think there is. You'll probably need to go to Nairobi for that."

"Yeah, that's what I figured."

"So what happened to his foot?"

"It was the craziest thing! He got a mosquito bite and scratched it until it got infected. At this point he can't even walk! We're just trying to find some antibiotics 'cause he's in pretty bad shape and needs something to fight the infection."

"Oh wow! Sucks mate! The disease here is nuts. What kind of antibiotics are you looking for?"

"Not sure. At this point, I'd try anything. You don't happen to have some laying around do you?" I said jokingly.

He thought for a moment. "Actually yeah, I've got some Cipro that you could have. Not sure if it'll work. Hell, it could even make it worse for all I know, but it is an antibiotic."

"Really? That would be great!"

"Okay, sure thing. Hey, wait here and I'll run up to my hotel and grab it. I'm just next door actually."

"That's great! I'll order us a couple more beers, on me."

"Cheers!" he said, as he walked out of the bar.

As I sat there it was hard to believe my luck. I found the only foreigner in town and he happened to have antibiotics that he was willing to just give away. Hopefully he came back…and hopefully the Cipro was safe…and hopefully it worked.

After about 10 minutes he came back and set a small bottle on the table.

"Ciprofloxicin 100 mg."
"Expiration Date: September 2009"

"Wow, this is great. Thanks so much!"

"Not a problem mate! And thanks for the beer."

"How much do you want for them?" I asked.

"Oh man, don't be crazy…on the house!"

"Oh are you sure?"

"Definitely! It's the backpackers code. Just pay it forward if you ever get the chance. I'm not gonna use 'em anyway."

"Well, okay. I can live with that!"

We finished our beers while discussing our travels in Africa and how it differed so much from the rest of the world. Although it wasn't long before Gareth decided that it was time for him to go to sleep. We parted ways and wished each other a safe journey. I immediately went back to the hotel and woke up Ethan.

"Dude! Wake up man! I've got some drugs for you!"

"Really? What did you get?"

"Cipro. I'm not sure if it will work or if it will kill you but at this point I think it's something we should consider."

Ethan looked over the bottle, asked how I got them and immediately popped the first pill. He had traveled in other countries before and had an instinct to trust fellow travelers.

"Well, let's hope this works," he said.

And we both went to bed a little nervous that night.

***

The next morning it was hard to tell if the pill had worked or not, but he wasn't dead so that was a plus. We made our way back to the main road and got on the first bus heading south to Nairobi. It was refreshing to be back in civilization where buses ran frequently. Unfortunately we were still on a rice and beans diet but no one was complaining.

After Ethan took his second pill we both began to settle in for the ride south in our nice, relatively comfortable bus to Nairobi. The journey was calm and predictable compared to what we had experienced further north, and that's exactly what we wanted.

It was a four-hour drive to Nairobi from Isiolo and at this point the countryside was all blurring together for me. I sat there staring out the window, not really understanding what I was looking at. More dirt, more trees, more villages...at this point I didn't care. I just wanted to get to Nairobi and find a doctor for Ethan. Then, get to a nice relaxing beach where I could enjoy a beer and stare at girls in bikinis. As the bus rolled on I fell asleep and began to dream about just that.

***

Hours later I gradually awoke to the smell of exhaust and the continuous sound of horns honking. From the bus window, I was able to look out onto a sea of chaos below me. Everywhere I looked I saw people, cars and motorcycles. There were rows upon rows of one and two story cement buildings that housed everything from corner stores to auto mechanics. As I looked out into the haze I could make out an address hand-written in paint above an open garage door. It read:

Skyline Motors Ltd
Muranga Road
Nairobi City, Kenya

The name of this business meant absolutely nothing to me except for its last line. We had finally arrived in Nairobi!

The bus had stopped at the central terminal in downtown Nairobi that just so happened to be the perfect place to catch the train east to Diani Beach. But first we needed to find a doctor for Ethan's foot.

"Hey man, wake up! We're in Nairobi," I said.

"Oh sweet! I need to get off this damn bus."

"So how's that foot doing?"

"Holy shit man!"

"What?" I replied.

"My foot. It's better...well, a little bit."

"Oh damn, that's great!" I said, with a sense of total relief. "We should still go find a doctor before heading to the beach though. I don't think there will be one once we get out there."

"What? No! It's fine now. I'm good. Let's just go. I

need some sun and cervezas after this last week."

"Are you insane? You could have lost your foot because of that infection. You still could! It still looks pretty damn bad. And don't you want to see Nairobi?" I said, trying to say anything to get him to agree to stay at least one night.

"Eh, to be honest, not really. I kinda just want to get to the beach."

All of a sudden he stopped what he was saying abruptly and began to stare off across the street. Through the traffic and the haze of smog I could see his eyes focusing on something in the distance.

"Oh shit! Is that a pizza place? I'll be right back."

Ethan dropped his bag and ran across the street towards a small pizza shop that looked like it was the Kenyan equivalent to Pizza Hut. He weaved his way around pedestrians and through the traffic as if he had lived his whole life in Nairobi. His foot was definitely looking as if it was better but I couldn't be sure. I knew the guy, and I knew what he was capable of doing for some food.

He shouted back, "See, look I can run now! It's really improving!"

I could only look back smiling as he ran toward the pizza place. People just do what they want. You can't change them.

After a moments pause, I yelled back, "Well, make it a large then!"

Ethan didn't like doctors, had his heart set on the beach and had just proved beyond a shadow of a doubt, in his mind, that he was 100% better. At this point there was no getting him to stay in Nairobi. So I bought a couple tickets for the night train east to Mombasa while he was getting the pizza. From Mombasa we would then need to travel south to Diani Beach, probably by matatu.

Ethan came strolling back with the biggest shit-eating grin on his face and carrying an extra large pizza in his right hand up high like a waiter. It was as if he had hunted that pizza down and killed it with his bare hands. He displayed the smug look of someone who just achieved something great. To be fair, he did find us pizza. So I'll give it to him.

We sat on a wooden bench on the platform of the train station as we ate our pizza. We still had an hour and a half before the train was scheduled to depart. Something about it felt absolutely amazing. Maybe it was because we were back in "civilization", maybe because the threat of Ethan's infected foot was nearly over, or maybe just because we had a delicious BBQ chicken pizza. Whatever it was it felt good to be in Nairobi, even if it was only for a few hours.

It was 4:30PM and the train arrived on schedule. This punctuality came as somewhat of a surprise to us based on our experiences over the last few days but we were now in the capital. Things worked better here. We boarded the train, took our seats and settled in. It was a comfortable ride with separate compartments for sleeping, probably a remnant from colonial days. It felt as if we were sitting in the seats of some upper class citizens who would eventually come and ask us to move.

As we slowly pulled away from train station, we could see Nairobi fading away behind us. From the city center we made our way east. As we traveled, the density diminished. Crowded streets gave way to the quieter roads of the African suburbs, business offices transformed into homes. Even further out we passed the slums with their tin roofs on the periphery of Nairobi's urban jungle, the last resort for the city's desperate countryside immigrants.

Further and further we traveled and eventually the city disappeared behind us. The countryside was simpler and quieter. From the comfort of the train it looked like a series of utopian villages where people enjoyed a simple and long-forgotten way of life. From the eyes of a jaded American, it looked as if they knew something we didn't, as if they were privy to a knowledge that we had forgotten.

Part of me wished that I could have had that life. I guess I could if I really wanted it, but everything looks better from the other side.

We both sat there quietly for nearly the entire trip, just enjoying the ease of travel and patiently waiting for our arrival in Mombasa. As we looked out on the tiny villages of east Kenya, we felt as if we were removed from it somehow. It was as if we weren't really there but watching it on television from a comfortable chair back home. National Geographic in high definition. It was a stark contrast to our previous two weeks of travel in the north where we easily felt connected, if only briefly, to the people and the places we visited.

As the train moved and hummed along, we both began to get sleepy. We closed the door to our sleeping compartment and tuned out for the rest of the night.

CHAPTER 21
BEACH BOUND

At around 5:30AM we arrived in Mombasa. Disoriented from being awakened at such an obscene hour, we stumbled out to the road from inside the train station. Before us was a new and different Kenya. We had arrived on the Swahili coast.

The Swahili culture developed as merchants from India and the Middle East arrived on the east African coast and set up trading settlements. Those imported customs then mixed with the local people to create a distinct new way of life, something unique in Africa. It was easy to see the difference here.

Everywhere we looked things were a little different. The food smelled spicier, the air carried that cool ocean mist and the architecture made us feel as if we had been dropped off in the middle of a historic old town center.

But the Muslim influence was the most noticeable. It traveled on the wind in the form of prayers being chanted from loudspeakers out of nearby Mosques. Men sat in outdoor cafés drinking tea from small glass cups while discussing the matters of the day. Women hustled about covered in full headdresses carrying groceries and chatting with one another. Somehow it had the flavor of India, Africa and the Middle East all within its streets.

Despite the new world that we had encountered, we didn't stay long. Within minutes of walking outside we were swarmed by the "bus-men" of Mombasa. It was their job to fill up the matatus with passengers and get them on the road as quickly as possible. A matatu couldn't leave unless it was filled to the brim with passengers. As we walked closer we could hear them yelling at the crowds of people passing by.

"Lamu! Lamu! Lamu!" yelled one man.

"Dar! Dar! Dar!" yelled another.

"Malindi! Malindi! Malindi!" from behind us.

As usual, we stuck out in the crowd and were immediately approached by one of the busmen. He knew all too well that tourists in this part of Kenya are only en route to a few select places. He approached us with intensity and a sense of urgency.

"My friends! Lamu?! Dar?! Diani?!" he asked us, expecting a prompt reply.

"Yes!" Ethan replied when he heard the word Diani. "We are going to Diani Beach."

"Ahh okay!" he grabbed me by the back of the arm and directed us to the end of a line of white matatus.

It looked exactly like all the others without any indication of where it might be headed, but he knew the system.

"Okay!" he said. "You can sit here," he pointed at the middle row of the matatu. "And your bags can go on top of you," he gestured towards his lap.

"Okay, thanks so much!" Ethan replied.

"Okay," he said in response, and walked away.

We both looked at each other as if we were unsure of what had just happened but it seemed to make sense. So we took our seats and sat with our bags on our laps as instructed.

As we waited for more people, the matatu began to heat up under the hot Swahili sun. Without any shade or breeze and our bags sitting on top of us, Ethan and I couldn't do anything but sit there and sweat. No one else seemed to mind. No one else seemed to sweat at all. It was again, a problem with us.

Luckily it wasn't long before our crew was assembled and we hit the road. The sweet sound of the engine turning over and the breeze beginning to pour through the vehicle clearing it of all its collected heat was an amazing moment. We were en route once again.

Mombasa sits on an island connected by roads to the north and ferries to the south. So from the city center we had to drive south where we loaded onto a ferry to cross Kilindini Port. Our matatu was able to pull right up onto the ferry without us even having to get out. Once aboard, we waited patiently as the ferry made its slow progression to the other side.

Back on the mainland it was an easy 30 kilometers south. Most of the drive hugged the coast with views of the great Indian Ocean at our side.

We could tell we were getting close by the salty smell in the air and the string of hotels that quickly started to pop up out of nowhere. All of a sudden the matatu stopped and everyone began to get out. This was our clue to do the same. As we looked around at the town before us it was hard to tell that we were anywhere close to a beach town. At first glance it looked like any non-descript small African town. But we had seen the hotels coming in and knew which way the ocean was. So without much thought, we started walking toward the direction of the water.

As we progressed down the dirt road heading towards the sand, we began to see signs for hotels and restaurants every few meters. One said, "Stilts" for a hotel that had built all its rooms on stilts above the ground. Another said "Forty Thieves" and mentioned cheap drinks and a beach bar. We were in the right place.

With each few steps our anticipation grew. The roofs of all the houses were now made of thatches rather than wood or tin. Below our feet we noticed that the rocks and gravel was slowly giving way to sand and within every few paces there would be an old coconut shell that had fallen from one of the palm trees above.

In the distance there was a small wooden sign in the shape of an arrow that pointed down a small sandy path to our left. It was nailed to a bamboo pole and written on that piece of wood was the one word we were looking for this whole time. That arrow-shaped sign simply read:

"Beach."

Without even a discussion of where to sleep or to put our bags, we began to follow that simple wooden sign. Through the sandy path between two huts, under the drooping palm leaves we stumbled blindly as the sand deepened underneath our feet. As we approached the end of the path we desperately climbed up from the bottom of a sand dune and looked out at what was before us.

There we stood, covered in sweat and staring straight ahead into the shallow turquoise waters of the Indian Ocean and the white sand beaches that had led us to it. In the distance we could see the waves casually washing up onto shore and the birds flying just above the surface of the water. To our left we saw two camels lying in the sand underneath the shade of a palm tree, and to our right was the Forty Thieves beach bar sitting right up against the sand, patiently waiting our arrival.

With only a couple of smiles between us and no words that needed to be spoken, we chose to make a right turn at that particular moment and leave our bags sitting right there in the sand.

A few moments later we arrived back to that spot where our bags were sitting, this time, with two large Tuskers and unbreakable sense of accomplishment. From our perfect seats in the white sand we could see the sun shining over that calm turquoise sea. We had arrived. After traveling through some of the harshest roads in Africa we had reached our paradise. And it felt amazing.

"So, how's the foot, better?"

"Look, the swelling is nearly gone!" he said, happy and

slightly bragging that his decision to avoid the doctor had paid off.

"Oh see, all you needed was a beer and some sand beneath your feet!" I said, while pausing for a moment.

"Very true," he replied, as he took a sip of beer.

"And…was it worth it?" I asked, cautiously.

"What, this long shitty trip of ours? Yeah, surprisingly it was. But it would have been so much easier just to fly," he said smiling.

"Yeah, but then what kind of story would you have?" I said defensively.

"Oh right! So you expect me to be a storyteller like Dad and those damn stories about grandpa?"

"Well you never know, someday, someone may actually want to hear one of your crappy stories."

"For sure," Ethan said, laughing. "Cheers to Dad…and Grandpa!"

"God! What is it with you and these cheesy toasts? Remind me to never let you speak at my wedding."

"Fine! Here's to the Watermelon King then."

"Deal."

Clink.

CHAPTER 22
THE AFTERMATH

Friday the 16th, February 2029. It started like any day before it. At 46 years old he had a pretty predicable routine in place. It was comfortable, normal and easy. He sat in his favorite chair staring at the glowing television mounted on the wall above him, relaxing after a long day at work.

From around the corner, his oldest daughter tears into the room with a stuffed teddy bear flailing in the air and crashes onto his lap with all the force she can muster.

"Ohhh my!" he shouts, in his best old-man voice. "What do you think you're doing?"

"Daddy, I'm bored! Where's mommy?"

"She's on her way home from work right now."

"Ahh, but I want her to make me something to eat!"

"Well, I can make something for you."

"No, Daddy, you don't know how!"

"Oh fine, then you'll just have to wait," he said, relieved.

"Daddy," his daughter said, changing the subject instantly as children often do. "Can you tell me a story?"

Ethan pauses for a moment as the question triggers something in his memory. He looks at his daughter and a smile begins to stretch across his face.

"Yeah, I think I've got one for you."

THE END

EPILOGUE

To this day, the *Watermelon Kingdom* is still in operation. It now goes by the name *Royse's Twin City Produce* and is owned and managed by Homer's daughter. It still sits on the same spot that it was originally founded on, and caters to much of the same clientele.

When Homer died in 2008 his wife left their house behind the fruit stand and moved closer to town to be near her loved ones.

Over the years more businesses began to build up around them; the property was eventually cleaned up and a new, and larger, storefront was built to modernize and expand the retail space.

Watermelons are still unloaded each week during the summer months, now with a new generation of expert stackers.

CONTACT

For more information on *The Watermelon King*, visit us online:

www.danielroyse.com
www.twitter.com/Royse_Daniel
www.facebook.com/DanielRoyseAuthor

ABOUT THE AUTHOR

Daniel Royse is the founder and editor in chief of the online travel publication, *This Boundless World*. He has written numerous articles on travel, business and politics. *The Watermelon King* is his first full-length novel.

Daniel is an obsessive writer and explorer who has backpacked to over 50 countries, spanning five continents. To the disbelief of many, he still enjoys long, hot bus rides through chaotic places.

DANIEL ROYSE

THE
WATERMELON
KING

BY

DANIEL ROYSE

Made in the USA
San Bernardino, CA
26 June 2018